Welcome

to MMA's Living Stewardship Series!

As a church-related organization dedicated to helping people live lives of Christian stewardship, MMA is pleased to provide this resource as part of the *Living Stewardship Series.*

MMA exists to help Christians answer God's call to care for and cultivate the gifts God has given them. To accomplish this, we offer products, services, and resources – like this study book. Our goal is to help you understand biblical principles of stewardship while, at the same time, providing real world ways you can incorporate those principles into your every day living.

The Bible tells us we are to seek wholeness in our lives. In the Gospel of Matthew (5:48) Jesus said in his Sermon on the Mount to *"Be perfect, therefore, as your heavenly Father is perfect."* But, who among us can ever be perfect?

Actually, the Greek word traditionally translated as "perfect" in that verse is *teleios* – which means, "to be whole." *Living Stewardship* is not a series for perfect people, but for people like you who are seeking wholeness. People who don't want to leave their faith in Christ at the church door after Sunday worship. People who want that faith to color how they relate to family and friends, how they work at their jobs, how they spend their money, how they take care of themselves – essentially, how they live.

At MMA, "holistic" refers to the essential interconnectedness of all the elements of Christian stewardship. For the sake of simplicity, we've identified the crucial elements as time, relationships, finances, health, and talents. Integrating all five, and nurturing the relationships between them, produces a healthy life of holistic stewardship. MMA feels strongly about holistic stewardship – so strongly, in fact, that we have reoriented our approach to stewardship to recognize this interconnectedness of all parts of our lives.

On the stewardship path of your life, you will find the journey easier if you pay attention to all of these areas of your life and recognize how they work together to lead you to the wholeness of God. If one of these elements becomes unbalanced, broken, or disconnected, you experience a lack of wholeness. However, with a strong core (faith) connecting each area, and careful attention to each area as needed, God's love can flow through you and produce wholeness in your life – and in the lives of others you touch.

What is MMA?

MMA is a church-related organization that helps Christians practice biblical stewardship.

We are the stewardship agency of Mennonite Church USA, but MMA also serves other faith communities affiliated with the Anabaptist tradition. MMA helps you pursue stewardship solutions through insurance and financial services, charitable giving, and other stewardship resources as well as with our educational resources, such as this study book, and stewardship education events through Stewardship University.

MMA wants to help you live a holistic life of stewardship centered on Christ — and become the best steward of God's resources you can.

This is why we believe *holistic stewardship* involves much more than just the products and services MMA provides. Holistic stewardship looks at the *interconnectedness* that weaves through the areas of our lives. And, as Christians, it's all filtered through our faith in Christ. This faith is what drives the search for wholeness.

How good a steward you are in your finances, can affect your health and your relationships. If you are having trouble with your health, that can affect how you are able to use your talents or your time each day. If you're overcommitted and your day feels too full, you may opt to give short shrift to your children or your job. And on it goes. There are countless ways our search for wholeness is affected by our shortcomings in these areas.

MMA®

Stewardship Solutions

Practical tips to keep you moving!

This study book is on money – but not just the ins and outs of budgeting. What you'll study in these pages is how money, and our stewardship of it, affects our lives and the lives of those around us. We live in a world of excess – but, we're surrounded by other cultures who struggle for daily bread. What does that mean to the Christian seeking God and wholeness?

But, because of the holistic nature of stewardship, don't be surprised when we also talk about your health, time, talents, and relationships – specifically as they relate to money.

We'll give you practical ways to implement the suggestions we make here – not just open-ended theories! Each chapter ends with discussion questions you can answer as a group, or individually, that will help you identify areas where you may need to do some repair work.

Finally, each book in this series will present you with an implementation plan that will help you identify some key steps you can take *right now*.

There's more!

If you like what you learn here, look for other study guides in the *Living Stewardship Series*.

If you want to learn more about us, visit MMA-online, our home on the Web (www.mma-online.org). There you can find more information and tools to help you on your stewardship journey. You'll also find connections to the MMA partners in your area who can help you achieve the stewardship goals you have for your life.

Money Mania
Mastering the Allure of Excess

by Mark L. Vincent

MMA®

Stewardship Solutions

Goshen, Indiana

Co-published with Herald Press

Money Mania

LivingStewardship Series

Unless otherwise indicated, all Scripture quotations are taken from the Holy Bible, New Living Translation, copyright 1996. Used by permission of Tyndale House Publishers, InCentury, Wheaton, Ill. 60189. All rights reserved. Other references are from New Century Version (NCV), Dallas: Word, 1991; New International Version (NIV), Grand Rapids: Zondervan, 1996; American Standard Version (ASV), Bellingham, Wash.: Libronix Corporation, Logos Research Systems, 2002.

Cover design by Tom Duckworth
Edited by Michael Ehret

MMA®

Stewardship Solutions

1110 North Main Street
Post Office Box 483
Goshen, IN 46527

Toll-free: (800) 348-7468
Telephone: (574) 533-9511
www.mma-online.org

Dedication

To my raven-haired dove. Breathe deep and sing.

Contents

First Word: Money Intersections

1   Your Household and Money —15

2   Giving First —25

3   Children and Money —35

4   Youth and Money —47

5   The Time Value of Money —57

6   Money and Stress —71

7   The Sandwich Generation —83

8   Living on Enough —95

9   An Alternative Retirement —105

10   Church and Money —117

11   Faith in the Marketplace —129

12   Finishing Well —139

Final Word: The Other Side —147

First Word: Money Intersections

It was a pleasure to write this book.

In addition to some of my own material, this book is packed with the talent MMA has assembled over the years. Thanks to Steve Ganger, Kelli Burkholder King, and Lynn Miller for material they provided. Thanks, particularly, to Steve for his ongoing support for this project in his role as MMA's Director of Stewardship Education. I must also thank my wife Lorie and our two children, Autumn and Zach. They have to live with the creative binges that accompany my writing style.

As you read this book you will visit various intersections of life – from establishing a household to distributing an estate. What you will learn here invites you to be earnest in your Christianity and to organize your household assets in ways that honor God. This is the aspiration of my life, and I encourage you to become a person who shares it.

An important Scripture walks with us throughout the book: 2 Corinthians 8:1-5. Sometimes it is front and center. Other times it is merely referred to. It is foundational.

The Offering

[1]Now, friends, I want to report on the surprising and generous ways in which God is working in the churches in Macedonia province. [2]Fierce troubles came down on the people of those churches, pushing them to the very limit. The trial exposed their true colors: They were incredibly happy, though desperately poor. The pressure triggered something totally unexpected: an outpouring of pure and generous gifts. [3]I was there and saw it for myself. They gave offerings of whatever they could – far more than they could afford! [4]Pleading for the privilege of helping out in the relief of poor Christians.

⁵This was totally spontaneous, entirely their own idea, and caught us completely off guard. What explains it was that they had first given themselves unreservedly to God and to us. The other giving simply flowed out of the purposes of God working in their lives.

(2 Corinthians 8:1-5; "The Message") Copyright © 1993, 1994, 1995, 1996, 2000, 2001, 2002 by Eugene H. Peterson.

Here we find a group of Christians from Macedonia who gave themselves to the Lord and then to the Apostle Paul's ministry. The result was an eagerness to financially participate in Paul's ministry. They actually pled with him to contribute to a relief effort for a suffering sister congregation. Their example invites us to consider whether we share their commitment – and whether we can make it the habit of a lifetime. The answer, of course, is yes – if we live within our means. Doing so helps us increase our cash flow, which in turn helps us increase in both assets and giving.

A final note: Not all of us live in healthy, extended, tender families like those advocated for in this book. Even if we do not, however, we can still create them. We simply cannot ignore the contribution that healthy families make in developing good community and economically sustainable lifestyles.

I invite you into these pages. Be challenged. Be strangely warmed by the breath of God. Be inspired to pledge all of your heart, soul, mind, and strength to the God of heaven. Yes, such a pledge includes money.

Why wouldn't it?

– Mark L. Vincent

Your Household and Money

A young couple, preparing for marriage, is seated at the bride-to-be's kitchen table. They are filling out a budget worksheet supplied by their pastor.

While filling it out, they discover they view money differently. Although both are conservative in their spending, she feels anxiety even talking about the subject. She wants everything to balance. "No debt" is her rule – even if it means long sacrifice. He is proud of his competence with money, however, and doesn't understand her anxiousness. He views their finances with greater optimism than she does and is willing to take a few risks. She doesn't want to know the details, just the bottom line. He relishes the reports his computer program spits out and spends time tweaking them. The bank balances are important, but secondary to him.

These differences mean the couple has the opportunity to be either wonderful complements to each other as they manage money for a lifetime – or to constantly be at odds. How they handle their differing perspectives will either be the source of a growing and rich relationship, or it will be a poison to consume their relationship. The fact is, brought together, their differing perspectives create a whole any Christian family is fortunate to have.

> *... differing perspectives create a whole any Christian family is fortunate to have.*

The importance of a balance sheet

A worksheet like the one our couple filled out begins with a balance sheet. Many households forget this step, because they start with their expenses and then try to earn enough money to pay them. That is, they try to get back to zero or a little above so all will be well.

This is where the young woman is coming from. She thinks filling out the budget worksheet will help them combine their respective financial obligations and incomes and that they might have to figure out what sacrifices to make so the bills get paid. Although her parents never talked openly about money, she knew they were still simmering in the debt they had accumulated for a new truck here, or an occasional vacation there. She has steeled herself for the bad news.

The young man is starting from a different place and is, perhaps, a bit more sophisticated in his approach. He thought they would begin by totalling income and would then deduct expenses, factor in their charitable contributions and savings, and seek to have a remainder at zero or above.

The problem with both of these approaches is that neither tracks the size of the estate. While the first hopes there can be some money to save, the second assumes some savings and even charitable giving will take place. Neither approach tells them whether or not they are solvent. Neither approach provides the tools necessary to manage the contingencies life is guaranteed to throw at them. In a few weeks this couple will promise to love each other – for richer or poorer. Without a balance sheet, they will never know which it truly is.

> *This couple will promise to love each other – for richer or poorer. Without a balance sheet, they will never know which it truly is.*

A balance sheet is a snapshot of a household's financial status. It compares liabilities (what they owe) versus assets (what they own). The larger the number on the positive side, the greater the potential to manage life's contingencies. The smaller the number gets, the less likely you are to be able to handle life as it comes.

For example: Family A has a combined income of $65,000 after taxes. Both spouses work full-time to earn this income. Expenses against this run nearly $65,000 as well. The house is mortgaged at 110 percent. There is a time-share on which the family makes monthly payments. Two car payments, credit cards, and one remaining education loan also drain their finances. As assets, they have an insurance policy with some money in the cash account, some retirement funds, and bank accounts – but the balance sheet indicates nearly two times the amount of liabilities as there are assets.

Family B has a combined income of $48,000 after taxes. One spouse works part-time from home in order to be with the children before and after school. Their expenses have been carefully trimmed to 65 percent of income. Charitable giving, savings, and what they call "running around money" makes up the rest.

Their home was purchased with a 20 percent down payment. They drive older cars for which they paid cash. Their one credit card is paid off monthly. Other assets include retirement funds, bank accounts, and some antiques picked up at rummage sales. The balance sheet indicates a positive number of almost a year's worth of family income.

If only income is reported, Family A looks far healthier financially. But, the balance sheets tell a different story.

Group questions

1. *What key lessons, good or bad, did you learn about money management growing up? What do you wish you had learned?*

2. *As you manage money now, who else is involved? Do you see money differently than they do? Where are you similar?*

3. *Read 2 Corinthians 8:3-5. Does this passage sound more like Family A or Family B? Why?*

Forming a spending plan that includes giving

I recommend when creating your balance sheets that you put "giving" as the first category of expenses. Even ahead of taxes. This surprises many Christians. Their family goes to church. They do some giving, but it remains undiscussed and certainly is not planned. So, why do I suggest this? Remember these words from Paul:

> "Entirely on their own they urgently pleaded with us for the privilege of sharing in this service to the saints. . . . they gave themselves first to the Lord and then to us in keeping with God's will." (2 Corinthians 8:3-5 NIV)

It is good for us to be deliberate in our giving, just as we are in our savings. Some families discover they must make adjustments if they want to give 10 percent as the worksheet recommends.

Let's return to our engaged couple. They show their worksheet to their pastor in a premarital counseling session. He tells them the purpose of keeping a balance sheet is to track whether they are moving upward in assets or not. This will help them manage any financial reversals. And there will be some, whether unemployment, medical bills, pregnancy leave, or returning to school. Knowing where their assets stand will offer this couple a different set of choices when difficulties or major adjustments come.

The pastor also talks about the need for a positive cash flow. A positive cash flow will help the couple build their assets, but only if they maintain the discipline of saving. Many opportunities for spending and "owning" will come their way, but only by spending less than they earn will they improve their cash flow. This is also known as "living within your means," or what Agur called our "daily bread" in Proverbs 30:8.

Finally, the pastor talks about the biblical instruction to "grow in giving," which comes from Scripture passages such as 2 Corinthians 8:3-5. He describes for them three benefits for those who grow in giving.

The first benefit

Giving is the clearest way to demonstrate God has first place in life. Not the government. Not our own desires. Not the obligations others – even family members – lay on us. Our engaged couple learns they are privileged people with significant purchasing power, especially if compared on a global scale. Their pastor also reminds them that those blessed with abundant resources are called to share abundantly, too (1 Timothy 6:18). They have the opportunity to leave the world a better place because they have been here.

Giving is a step forward in spiritual maturity. Our young couple is challenged to take a step of faith by increasing their giving and trusting God to meet their needs. Many of us think this is difficult to do, but the ability to give "first to the Lord" might merely require dining out less often or dropping our subscription to cable or satellite television.

> *The ability to give "first to the Lord" might merely require dining out less.*

The second benefit

Growing in giving adds to the quality of life. A few years ago, a man named Douglas Lawson wrote a book called "Give to Live: How Giving can Change Your Life" (1999, ALTI Publishing). In it Lawson listed the benefits and additions to life enjoyed by those who choose to be generous. Here is his list:

Physical benefits

- Greater longevity.

- Significant reduction in toxic stress chemicals in the body (and so less stress).

- Enhanced functioning of the immune system.

- Decreased metabolic rate.

- Improved cardiovascular circulation.

- Healthier sleep.

- Help in maintaining good health.

Emotional benefits

- Increased self-acceptance.

- Reduced self-absorption and sense of isolation.

- Increased endorphin release (which provides a natural emotional "high").

- Expanded sense of control over one's life and circumstances.

- Increased ability to cope with crises.

- Stronger feelings of personal satisfaction.

- Improved concentration and enjoyment of experiences.

- Enhanced compassion, empathy, and sensitivity to others.

- Reduced inner stress and conflict.

Spiritual benefits

- Greater connectedness to God.

- More receptivity to spiritual guidance.

- Added involvement in charitable activity.

- Heightened sense of appreciation and acceptance of others.

- Sustained peace of mind.

- Greater clarity about the meaning and purpose of life.

- Enhanced quality of life.

The third benefit

Giving leads to an increase in assets. When people give, it orients them toward God, God's work in the world, and others. They begin to set aside time and finances to invest in family, friends, neighbors, church, and even the global community. The result is a much larger circle of friends and family than they would have otherwise and they live out the blessing of Genesis 12:2-3.

Imagine again our engaged couple experiencing job loss or a prolonged illness. Would they rather face it as people who chose a consumer-oriented lifestyle and few true friends, or as people who chose a giving-oriented lifestyle with a large network of a faith-based family? It's a pretty simple answer.

Giving first to the Lord also strengthens the habit of giving "second to savings." Get these two habits (giving and saving) in place and assets and cash flow increase even faster, providing opportunities to give even more. What a wonderful life adventure our engaged couple, and we, could have if this is how we choose to orient our lives.

Prayer:

God, help us to understand the way we approach and handle money as a gift from you. Some of us are created one way, and some another. Together we complement each other and lead each other to a deeper experience of your love. Help us, also, Lord to approach our finances with a giving orientation rather than an orientation built on consuming. Help us to learn that blessing others brings your blessing on us.

Amen.

End questions

Consider your own spending plan:

1. Do you have more month at the end of your money or more money at the end of the month?

2. If you ever find yourself in a tough spot with your household budget, who might you talk to for guidance? Why?

3. How would you evaluate the giving factor in your life? Read James 1:17. What does this tell you about the source of the gifts we are able to give?

Giving First

Reflecting again on 2 Corinthians 8:1-7, a family wanting to live from an orientation toward giving might begin to use the following table prayer when they sit down to eat:

Dear Lord, in all our lives we want to first give to you, then to others. May the good cooking and warm fellowship around this table inspire us in service for you. In Jesus' name, Amen.

"First to the Lord" echoes pretty loudly. "First to the Lord" means the *first* check and the *first* amount is paid, even if it means sacrificing other things. It is a wonderful way to live. Doing it is not obligation. Instead, it is a hymn of praise to the God who provides (2 Corinthians 9:6-7).

Setting goals

Giving first to the Lord is a central goal for any Christian family. Adopting this goal means more than just admitting it is a nice value to have. Rather, giving first to God is the pivot point around which the rest of our financial management rotates. Even the family estate becomes a statement of giving. By setting goals and making plans, a family can continue giving – especially to those places that received a significant investment from them already.

In 2004, the Evangelical Lutheran Church in America published a book I co-wrote with Michael Meier called "The Whys and Hows of Money Leadership" (Augsburg Press, 2004). The book was written for pastors in their first congregation and taught a percentage-based method for managing money. Older adults would notice almost immediately that this style of management is similar to the envelope system they or their parents may have used.

People use bank accounts and computer programs now, so instead of real envelopes, a family can be percentage-based by thinking about the way they allocate their money.

This system encourages you to think about the distinction between what you need – the "providing" expense – and what you want – the "consuming" expense. Many other systems don't make this distinction.

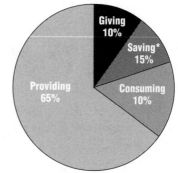

Adult income allocation chart
*10% for long-term savings, 5% for short-term savings, which creates a cash reserve, worth 4-6 months' income.

For instance, I need transportation. But, I don't necessarily need a particular car, or even a car. I need clothing. But, I don't need 20 shirts. This is the distinction made between providing and consuming. The percentages listed in the allocations in the pie chart are only principles, but they come pretty close to a healthy average in most regions of the United States. Further, they remind you that you only have 100 percent of what you have. You certainly don't have 103 percent. Households that get into financial trouble seem to think they do, however, and they spend more than 100 percent of their money on a regular basis. The result is stress, crisis, and fear.

A family can be percentage-based by thinking about the way they allocate their money.

Getting your allocations in order and maintaining them not only helps you avoid debtors' crush (Proverbs 22:7), it also helps you live a well-rounded life. Interestingly, the consuming part, what older generations call "walking-around money," also needs to be set aside, just like savings and giving.

Let's say a family has $50,000 to work with after taxes. That's more than many families make, but it is a nice round number to work with. If they start by allocating 10 percent of that for giving, they will have $5,000 to distribute. If they then allocate 15 percent of their income for saving, they will put aside $7,500 per year. Of course, they will want to divide it up between short- and long-term savings, so let's say 10 percent to long-term and 5 percent to short-term. Short-term is a cash savings account of some kind that they can get at more quickly if they need it. Long-term savings is what they set aside for their retirement.

Their allocation for their consuming expenses assumes they will also benefit from setting aside 10 percent of their income for the things they enjoy. The key is that doing so creates a limit – and very few people are willing to limit their spending on wants to 10 percent of their income – most of us want to allow room for "more." However, by establishing the limit from the beginning, the family is less likely to eat into the money needed for the mortgage, utilities, basic clothing, groceries, or medicine.

> *The key is that doing so creates a limit – and very few people are willing to limit their spending.*

So, let's go over this again. Our test family earns $50,000 after taxes, gives away $5,000, saves $7,500, and sets aside another $5,000 for the fun stuff like gift giving, vacations, or eating out. That leaves them $32,500 – which covers their providing expenses, such as a house payment and groceries.

Can you see how that limits appetite? Many families work with a real estate agent or buy a car based on all of their after-tax income, instead of their income after these set-asides. Imagine the difference in perspective of what a family can afford when they put giving and saving first – and then set limits on their consumptive habits! Our family is going to look for houses they can afford on $32,500, rather than on their income of $50,000.

When a family does the reverse – starting with the house and cars it wants – and then tries to figure out its giving and saving goals after expenses are set, they often find they're pinched. Many American families don't want to reduce what they consume, so naturally giving and saving both disappear. The result is no assets and no improving cash flow for the family.

Two more thoughts

Let's make a couple more observations about this way of allocating money. The first is the idea of a cash reserve. If our family doesn't have some sort of savings account, they end up borrowing money, not saving, or not giving in order to cover any emergency they may face. Their 5 percent short-term savings rate is what helps them build a modest cash reserve they can use if they have to replace a refrigerator unexpectedly or have a sudden medical expense.

It is good for a family to have four months or more of income on hand to cover these emergencies, especially in these days of employment uncertainty. Once they fund their reserve, the family can distribute leftover money to other things. They could spread it evenly across their other allocations – or they could choose to increase their giving. Of course, they could also choose to purchase something they delayed buying until now.

The second observation is that they should drive a lifestyle stake and say "this is enough – this and no more." If they do, their consuming and providing, and perhaps even their saving percentages, can go down, while giving increases to their congregation and other ministries.

Group questions

1. Think about how you allocate your income. How do your percentages differ from those of our imaginary family? What adjustments are you willing to make so that your percentages break down more realistically?

2. Are you prepared to drive a lifestyle stake at this time? If not, what more do you require?

3. Re-read 2 Corinthians 8:1-7. What are the connections between your giving and how you manage money?

Why percentages?

In my teaching of percentage-based money management for households and con-gregations, people regularly ask why I do this instead of talking about specific amounts. One important reason is that some of us are not very good at numbers. It's not natural for many of us to be precise when figures are mentioned with no anchoring point of reference. We get lost.

Talking in percentages is just as accurate, but also provides an anchoring ref-erence point. We simply are better able to communicate in units of one hundred, or as pieces of a pie, especially when trying to manage money in a group such as a family or a congregation.

In the book, "The Millionaire Next Door" (Thomas J. Stanley, Ph.D., William D. Danko, Ph.D. Marietta, GA: Longstreet Press, 1996), the authors wrote that many wealthy people don't budget at all, but follow a "pay themselves first strategy" (p.41). The millionaires in the study weren't particularly generous, but the strategy of saving and making other payments before spending on themselves is pretty much what our chart shows. The good news is that you don't have to be an accounting wiz to grow your assets. We simply have to understand how much is available to us and make sure the important things are paid *first*.

> *We simply have to understand how much is available to us and make sure the important things are paid first.*

This is not to encourage you toward millionaire-dom. The book was merely a sociological study of millionaires who have most of their money tied up in their businesses. They don't have it in their bank accounts. Most of them didn't set out to be millionaires, either. They simply wanted to run a successful business and be prudent money managers. Becoming a millionaire was a side benefit. Most people are like this. They will never see the result of their savings until they retire – and then only if they have a good succession plan as well.

The World War II generation lives this way. Overall, they are frugal with them-selves and very generous toward their churches and communities. The result of their frugality is that they don't spend all their money. This makes generosity possible and increases their circle of friends. People in business who live in this way also have many friends and improve their chances for success. If they continue in the combination of frugality and generosity, the circle increases yet again, bringing larger sums of money into their life.

Think back on our engaged couple from Chapter 1. Remember the three areas of growth – assets, cash flow, and giving? If they grow in cash flow and assets, they can also grow in giving. As they grow in giving, they are *likely* also to grow in cash flow and assets.

If they continue in the combination of frugality and generosity, the circle increases yet again, bringing larger sums of money into their life.

Accumulating cash flow and assets in order to be generous is not a selfish way to live. Those who spend all of their income are the ones investing in a selfish lifestyle. They spend everything they have (and often more) on themselves, then have nothing left over to give to God or community.

If we don't increase our giving all through our lives, we will only count what we stored (or failed to store) instead of what we gave. The challenge, of course, is to grow in generosity toward God when our capacity is limited by suffering – just as we increased our generosity when we were in plenty.

Prayer:

Most generous Lord, we come before you with our lives open in all ways.
We look around us and see all that you have provided – and we are grateful!
Help us, God, to give first back to you, reflecting the generosity we see in you.
Be with us as we contemplate the significant difference between our wants
and our needs – and help us to recognize those differences. Bless our
decision to be responsible with the gifts you have given.
Amen.

End questions

1. How do you think communicating in percentages helps people with different styles work together in managing money?

2. Have you benefited from the generosity of the World War II generation in some way? How? What might you do to continue their legacy of giving?

3. Read Psalm 37:21 and Psalm 50:10. What do these passages tell us about true ownership of resources? Then, read 1 Corinthians 4:1-2. What is our God-appointed role in relationship to money?

Children and Money

Most Christian parents affirm they want to teach their children to love God more than money. But many are unclear how to do so.

How do we teach this priority when giving an allowance? Are there teachable moments when our children begin to discover the power of money to give them what they want? Many of us worry more about how to get our kids to stop begging for money than how to pass on to them a set of spiritual values concerning money, generosity, and wealth.

Consider two stories from Scripture. In the first, Abraham distributes his estate — and his sons. In the second, a loving father gives everything he has to both of his sons.

Genesis 25:1-6

These verses are full of names we are tempted to overlook because we can barely pronounce them. But in these words, we read that Abraham distributed his estate to his sons and scattered them to live as resident aliens in far lands — as he had been. By scattering them instead of letting them become a tribe that could protect itself, Abraham's sons, especially Isaac, would have to learn to live trusting in God's provision. To Abraham, this was more important than keeping his wealth under the control of a clan.

Luke 15

In the story of the Prodigal Son, the loving father did not withhold the family estate from his younger son — or, for that matter, from his older indignant son who thought his father was showing favoritism. What the father had was fully available to both of his boys. His estate became a tool used to teach love and forgiveness.

In both stories the parent uses an inheritance to teach character. The end the parent has in mind is *not* the preservation of the family endowment, but the preservation of the family values. Jesus uses the story of the loving father and his prodigal son to teach us that God operates this way with us as well. God uses the endowment of creation to teach us to love him with all our heart, our soul, our mind, and our strength (Luke 10:27).

> *God uses the endowment of creation to teach us to love him with all our heart, our soul, our mind, and our strength.*

Battle for souls

All of us, parents and grandparents, must learn to keep the main thing the main thing when teaching our children about a relationship with God. The main thing is that our children learn to love God with all their heart, soul, mind, and strength. We want them to enter adulthood belonging fully to God and not to something less. You can give children an allowance, and even teach them to tithe, but still fail to teach them the importance of *belonging to God*. The good news is that you can't teach them to belong fully to God without also teaching them about living a balanced life, about being generous, and about taking care of God's world.

Look at the chart that follows. This list comes from several Canadian denominations that combined their efforts and is adapted from "Planting Seeds of Faith: Growing Generous Hearts" (used with permission). These denominations wanted to develop a common educational plan to teach children about money. They want children coming up through the families of their congregations to know that a generous God gives them everything they have – and that the best way they can fulfill their purpose as God's creation is through lifelong generosity.

The list is broken down by the ages and stages of childhood, from infants to 18. You may notice that it talks about money – a little – but emphasizes the larger theme of appreciating God's gifts and becoming a generous person in response. Each resource event and gift in the "church" column is an opportunity to remind children (and their parents) to live a generous life toward God in response.

Growing generous hearts

Age	Stage in growing a generous heart	What the church can do
Infancy	Celebrating God's gift of life	Event: Baby's first Sunday Parent-child dedication Gift idea: Blanket
2-4 years	Nurturing a spirit of gratitude	Event: "Meet your Sunday school teacher" night Gift idea: Book
5 years	Learning to share	Event: Resource event for parents Gift idea: Pocket stone and Bible story book
8 years	Caring for God's creation	Event: Resource event for parents Children's club sleepover Gift idea: CD
12 years	Stewards of self, time, and talents	Event: Resource event for parents Gift idea: Signed and marked Bible
16 years	Including God as I make choices	Event: Resource event for parents Gift idea: Key chain
18 years	Partnering with God	Event: Celebration of child's birthday Gift idea: Comforter

Take a moment to think about some family activities of your own. Here are some examples:

One family attaches a small gold clip to their wallets. There is a cross on the clip. Each time they use their wallets, they see the cross of Jesus. Their children were given these crosses when they got their first job after college or trade school. The crosses are meant to be a consistent reminder that they are God-followers.

Some might consider using the cross in this way theologically offensive. But the important concept is finding ways to involve the unique heritage of your family. What symbols convey the power of your commitments? What is meaningful for you?

In many Latino families, a child's 15th birthday is of greater importance than the 16th. These celebrations, especially for a young woman, are called a *quincenera* and are a combination birthday and coming out party. But the party also marks a commitment to sexual purity and to giving one's self only to a spouse. Some Latino families now emphasize this for young men also – a *quincenero*. These celebrations are a natural part of their family traditions. What fits with yours?

In our home, our children began earning an income with their assigned chores after their 13th birthday. We pay them a little more than minimum wage and require that they give 10 percent to the Lord and save 50 percent or more for their future education. They are then free to use the rest to pay for extra clothing they want, entertainment opportunities, or other things they just have to have. Amazingly, our children often choose to go without rather than spend their hard-earned money frivolously. Does our tradition give you any ideas?

Group questions

1. *How did your parents handle the allowance issue?*

2. *How did, or will, you handle the issue with your children?*

3. *Evaluate the list of activities suggested for churches on the chart. Do you agree with the activities listed there? Why or why not?*

4. *On a separate piece of paper, write down several family traditions from your childhood. Add to this list traditions your current household has developed. Don't worry about connections to teaching children about money at this point. Simply make the list for later reference. (If married, compare your list with your spouse's – or have him or her help you with your list.)*

No guilt

Some families hand down no traditions, or the ones they do hand down are dysfunctional and destructive. Other families create traditions their children do not wish to continue. The good news is you are not bound by anyone's traditions, or anyone else's demands. Guilt does not move anyone toward joy. Joy comes from having the freedom to choose a tradition – and watch the lesson of it unfold in the life of a child as he or she picks up Godly character traits.

Guilt does not move anyone toward joy.

Maybe you will choose to plant a tree when your children are born. Maybe you will give a 4-year-old his $1 allowance in 10 dimes so he can begin to learn about dividing money between giving, saving, and various types of spending. Maybe you will buy your daughter a children's story about generosity toward God and others for her to learn as she reads. Maybe you will need to think of new activities for your older children, as you cycle back to get family traditions underway with the younger ones. Maybe you're not a parent, but your position of influence is that of a family friend, mentor, uncle or aunt, or a grandparent. Take delight in figuring out how to nurture the generosity of the children in your life.

There are many wonderful ideas, but no one family can do them all. The point is to have some meaningful traditions built around the important qualities you want your children to gain. They don't learn these qualities by accident – and we cannot teach them only with good intentions.

Four keys to teaching generosity

Consider the following four keys when teaching generosity to children. These lessons are condensed from the *Stewardship for Kids* series available as free downloads from MMA through MMA-online (www.mma-online.org).

Key One: When children are little, teach them to say prayers of thank you to God. It isn't hard for children to tell God what they want or to ask God for help. Children do that instinctively. Learning to say thank you as the main focus of prayer, however, takes practice. The practice starts with parents praying in this way, then teaching their children to be thankful as well.

Key Two: Invite them to give generously throughout their lives. Use pennies with the youngest children and move into larger amounts as they grow. Expect them to give 10 percent of whatever small allowance they are given – and then to give 10 percent of their pay when they get their first jobs. Expect them to give even when they are in college and hardly have any money and you are still supporting them. Describe giving as a way to worship God rather than an obligatory payment.

Combined with this habit of giving, expect your children to save 50 percent of anything they earn while living in your home. This may be hard for them when their friends have more CDs, more video games, or their own cars. But, by saving 50 percent from junior high through college, the average young person can pay cash for two years of their college education – rather than have to borrow that money. The other teens may have to sell their cars and borrow funds in order to get an education. This habit of saving also helps your child avoid significant debt as he or she enters adulthood. As a result, your children will have a greater ability to give to God's work, both now and as they think about what they will do as they approach retirement.

Key Three: Teach your child to give more than just money and to give to places other than just the church (Proverbs 3:27-28). If you aren't bound up in debt, you don't have to work extra hours or waste time in worry. This frees up time you can invest in other ways – for instance, attending your children's activities, serving as a coach for one of their teams, serving at a soup kitchen, or teaching Sunday school.

Key Four: This last section is critical: Teach your children about limits and choices. The money you have is the money you have, and the money they have is the money they have. There is a limit. The money you have must cover your needs before you use it to pay for your wants. Groceries before bicycles. Gas in the car is a higher priority than a second pair of shoes. A magazine from the library is a better choice than a magazine from the store.

When your child pushes you to buy something he or she wants, present it as a choice. For instance, pretend your 14-year-old son wants to snow ski. No one in your family skis. You have no ski equipment in your home. None of your neighbors ski. You live nowhere near a ski resort. Still, your son asks many times. Do not tell him no. Do not tell him yes. Give him a choice.

Make a list of items your son would like that are similar in value: a better bicycle, guitar lessons, going to camp with a friend. Make certain the list reflects the amount you are willing to contribute, if any, so your son understands how much of his own money would be required to fulfill his desire. Then let him choose which he wants. Giving him freedom to choose lets him explore his interests without exceeding your limits. Even when he chooses something other than your preference for him, he is learning to live within limits, while exploring his horizons.

And, if your son saves up the money for the ski trip (in addition to his giving to the Lord and any other financial obligations), I would encourage you to find a way to congratulate him on his dedication and discipline – and get him to the slopes! But, even if he chooses one of the other options, he is still learning that getting what he desires requires discipline – and teaching discipline to our children is one of God's highest priorities (Proverbs 13:24).

Even when he chooses something other than your preference for him, he is learning to live within limits, while exploring his horizons.

A typical response to this suggestion is that it cannot possibly work. I am often told children must be directed, that parents should not be so ready to give up control, or that "I could never take a risk like that." I'm afraid these parents will go on wondering why their children do not take responsibility for their actions, while those who offer their children choices – within limits – will teach them to be wise and generous managers of money.

Prayer:

Lord, our children are among the best gifts you have given us. We desire to teach them generosity in ways that will both encourage generosity in them and honor you. Help us teach the children in our lives to love you with all their heart, soul, body, and mind – and that doing so revolves around generous living. And help us to be generous to them in giving of ourselves.

Amen.

End questions

1. *Are you practicing the key ideas in this chapter? Are you teaching them to the children in your life?*

2. *What is the next step for you in giving all through your life?*

3. *Are you giving in ways other than money and in places other than church? Is this a value you are teaching to the children in your life? If not, how can you begin doing this?*

Note: In cooperation with Nathan Dungan and his Share-Save-Spend organization, MMA is now offering the Share-Save-Spend youth curriculum. This curriculum kit will help you teach children in your church about God-honoring financial habits. Nathan is the author of "Prodigal Sons and Material Girls: How Not to be Your Child's ATM." See MMA-online (www.mma-online.org) for details.

Youth and Money

Scene One – The Shema

Ancient Israel believed it was appropriate to discuss beliefs and values with children. In Deuteronomy 6:1-9, it is stated that love for God and affection for God's way was to be discussed in the home, while out walking, when lying down at night, and when rising again in the morning. Love for God's way was to be visible in the home, and in the lives of both parents and children. Successful parenting was the transmission of love for God from parent to child.

Scene Two – The Benedictus

In Luke's gospel, the priest Zechariah sings a lovely song at the ceremony that named his son John (Luke 1: 67-80). His song, which the Catholic church has called "The Benedictus," includes lyrics that celebrate a new unity between father and son that would ultimately be achieved in the work of Jesus, the Messiah. This is ironic since Jesus pointed out his ministry would sometimes divide family relationships rather than unite them (Matthew 19:29; Luke 14:26). Still, Zechariah's priestly vision of the Messiah's work lines up with Paul's instructions that parents in the early church must pass their values to their children (Ephesians 6:4). In this way, hope in God is more certain to continue as a family heritage.

Scene Three – Lois, Eunice, and Timothy

The Apostle Paul had a protege named Timothy. In a letter to him, Paul celebrates how Christian values had been present in three generations of Timothy's home (2 Timothy 1:5). Paul also spends considerable time telling Timothy how he must also pass these values along to the spiritual children he was responsible for. One group Timothy was to instruct were those "rich in this present age." He was to teach them to place their hope in the life to come. To be generous and ready to share (1 Timothy 6:17-19).

Scene Four – My own home

As I reached my teenage years, my father did two things for me. First, he brought me into the family's household budget management. He made me his assistant in balancing the family checkbook. This small act made money something real, something limited, and something I could understand. I learned what it took to cover household expenses, and I also learned what our family gave to the Lord in worship.

Second, my father made it clear I would now be more responsible for my own expenses. There would be food on the table for me, clothes for school and church, and a roof over my head. They would even provide me with a modest allowance. Any other money I wanted to spend and any future plans for education were up to me. My parents would provide counsel. They would coach me toward certain outcomes. They might even be able to help a little, but I should expect to bear the responsibility for earning my own way.

Back to the chart

Let's return to the money allocations chart from Chapter 2.

Remember, it works like the envelope budgeting system where you take your cash and divide it into envelopes for groceries, for utilities, for giving, for saving – that sort of thing. Since many people use checking accounts now, we need a variation of the envelope method to do the same thing. The percentages are pretty much the same for any household, regardless of income. However, higher income earning people might wish to give or save more because they don't have to take as high a percentage of income to provide for their household.

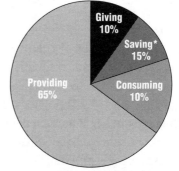

Adult income allocation chart
*10% for long-term savings, 5% for short-term savings, which creates a cash reserve, worth 4-6 months' income.

Provision is taking care of the basics – housing, clothing, medicine, groceries, reliable transportation. This is different from consumption expenses like entertainment, clothing you don't need, a car stereo, gift giving, or eating out. Many people do not distinguish between the costs to provide for their household and the costs of doing fun things. They're not willing to limit their fun, so they overspend. They cover their ears to the total and hide their eyes, hoping it will all work out by the end of the month without doing the math.

Unfortunately, some Christian-based money management systems do not make this distinction either. They might talk about "giving, saving, and spending," but the "spending" part of things is not divided between needs and wants. As a result, grabbing a soda at the convenience store is treated equally with buying groceries. Going out to eat is treated equally with paying for medical prescriptions. The result is poor habits, which are transmitted to children as readily as good ones – possibly even more so.

> *Provision is taking care of the basics – housing, clothing, medicine, groceries, reliable transportation.*

Additionally, young people – and their parents – do not learn to be exact. They are good people – good people who keep getting into financial trouble. The money allocation chart can help them understand how to divide their money by percentages. Consequently, they are reminded that they only have 100 percent of what they have. It is amazing how many do not want to hear this truth. Since most are not accountants, they throw up their hands and pretend there is nothing they can do.

Since it is difficult for many people to measure their money exactly, allocating their money in this way helps them become effective even if in a less precise manner. Everyone can count to four. Rather than putting energy into precise money management, energy is put into financial discipline. The discipline is to *not* spend money allocated for one thing on another.

Group questions

1. *What values are you intentionally passing along to the youth or other mentoring relationships in your life?*

2. *Do any of these values involve money? If so, what are they? If not, why not?*

3. *How much is your 100 percent? How is your 100 percent allocated to giving, saving, providing, and consuming? How does this correspond to the percentages in the chart?*

What I like about thinking about money in allocations, is that it helps us consider what we want to spend on fun things instead of telling us we have to deny ourselves. Yes, we have to set – *and honor* – limits, but we can still have fun! Start your budget process with what you will give. Expand to include what you will save and what you will spend to have fun. Then, take the 65 percent or so that should remain to pay for your housing, transportation, and grocery needs.

When you meet with a real estate agent and begin searching for a home, the agent is going to ask you how much you earn to determine the amount of house you can afford. If your income is $50,000, he or she will try to sell you a house that costs $150,000 – or more. But, this would be backward because your house payment would then determine what you allocate to the other categories of giving, saving, and consuming. If you decide on the car you want in the same way, I can pretty much guarantee that after paying a mortgage and a car payment you will not be able to give or save or consume at the percentages shown on the chart.

Is there another way to do these things? Here's an idea: What if you talked to the agent and the car salesperson *after* you took time to set aside money to give, money to save, and money for things you enjoy? Then, when you talk to the agent, tell her the income you have available is $32,500 (65 percent of a $50,000 income). You may see houses that are disappointing to a materialistic dream, but you will be able to afford not only a house, but also a vacation, birthday gifts, and an occasional meal in a restaurant – and you'll retain the ability to do it next year, too.

Houses cost a lot more than $150,000 in many places, such as California. That's part of the reason why more children are living with their parents now before they purchase a home of their own. That's also why many families are in financial trouble – they wanted a house and they tried to work everything out afterwards. But since they aren't saving enough, they are spending themselves into a hole. They don't want to deny themselves the fun things of life, but as a result they have no ability to manage life's contingencies.

Connecting this wisdom to young adults

With this background in mind, let's talk about how to transmit these values to youth. While the money allocations categories remain the same for teens, the percentages are different.

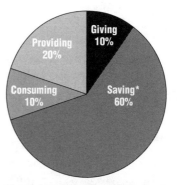

It is good for a young person to develop the habit of giving from the first moment they begin earning – whether their earnings come from an allowance or a paper route. If you expect your child to pay the majority of their college costs, they will likely need to save the majority of any income they make. However, even if they save 60 percent of what they earn from junior high through their senior year of college, they will be

Youth income allocation chart
*55% for long-term savings, 5% for short-term savings, which creates a cash reserve, worth 4-6 months' income.

fortunate if they have enough saved for two years of college. The rest would still have to be financed in some way or parents would need to match their child's savings to help them avoid borrowing for higher education.

Another question parents often face is whether to give their child a car or insist they purchase it from their earnings. Realistically, it is of little help for your teen to have transportation if, when they graduate from college, they have a debt equivalent to their first year of income. If, however, they save at a 60-percent rate, they will barely have enough left over to put gas in the family car let alone waste it on frivolous things. But, the good news is your children will understand both the power and the limitations of money.

It isn't that they can't do fun things, they just have to limit themselves – like you, their parents. If they don't learn to do this, there will be no giving, no saving, and no ability to make adjustments when something unexpected comes along. In the end, the amount of allowance your children earn doesn't matter nearly as much as the discipline they learn from living within their means.

> *The amount of allowance … doesn't matter nearly as much as the discipline they learn from living within their means.*

Young people need to establish a cash reserve as well. Let's put it in the context of a young person about to go to college. He is working all summer and has access to a car his uncle has loaned him. All he has to do is put gas in and cover any repairs. Sweet deal. But the battery goes dead because he left the lights on and now he has to replace it. Where will that money come from if he doesn't have a reserve?

To keep the cash reserve fund separate, consider putting 5 percent of the money earned into a savings account. Even at this rate, the teen will need several years to save enough to have a month or two of income on hand. The other 55 percent of money being saved can be put into a longer-term savings instrument. This is money they do not touch until they are ready for college.

All this is, of course, in general terms. Your family situation might mean your son or daughter can save more – or less. Maybe you want your child to have more experiences as a young person. Then you may choose to pay for some of their consumptive items, such as a week or two at church camp. Maybe you think they should pay all their costs – maybe none. It's up to you. But decide the formula you will use. It needs to be realistic and consistent and ought to communicate your values as a Christian. Don't wait until your child becomes a teenager – begin now.

Your children need to understand their economic limits and live within them. Doing so will bring them much more financial freedom. Building one's assets and the ability to give come from improved cash flow. There are no exceptions. May your children learn these lessons from you – and may they grow up to say "thank you" by passing these same values to their own children, as Christians are instructed to do in Deuteronomy 6:1-9.

Prayer:

Lord, help us to live out the values we long for our children to embrace. May they see in us a sincere desire to give generously, manage wisely, and plan prudently. Help them grow up with a healthy understanding of money, neither fearing nor revering it. For only you are worthy of our praise and allegiance. May we be the models for them as Jesus has been for all of us.

Amen.

End questions

1. *How did you manage money when you were young? What were your successes and failures?*

2. *What are your expectations for the young people in your home?*

3. *What is the savings rate of the children and/or grandchildren in your life? Do you intend to contribute to any college/vocational training they need? How much? Will it cover the cost? If not, how will the deficit be covered?*

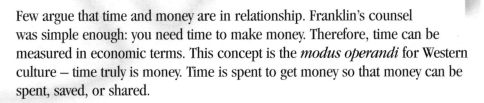

The Time Value of Money[1]

"Remember that time is money. Money can beget money, and its offspring can beget more. The way to wealth is ... waste neither time nor money."[2]
– *Benjamin Franklin*

Few argue that time and money are in relationship. Franklin's counsel was simple enough: you need time to make money. Therefore, time can be measured in economic terms. This concept is the *modus operandi* for Western culture – time truly is money. Time is spent to get money so that money can be spent, saved, or shared.

Why else do we so often hear Westerners say, "This is a waste of my time?" The growth of the professional services industry is a leading indicator. Mowing my own lawn is a waste of time; I'll hire someone else to do it for me. Grocery shopping? No, I'll order online and have it delivered. Why? Because we often believe we can use those precious hours to do something more productive – something that will generate more income. Or, if not generating income, then spending the income we've accumulated. Of course, we don't say it that bluntly, but the underlying motivation is centered upon Franklin's idea that it is wasteful to use time for something other than earning money. Non-economic uses of time are not valuable in this model.

Not a worldwide concept

Interestingly, much of the rest of the world has a different take on time and money. In Eastern and Southern cultures, the focus reverses. Westerners measure time in economic terms. People in Eastern and Southern cultures *compare* economic impact in terms of time. In our actions Westerners say, "It isn't worth my time." Other cultures say, "My time isn't worth it."

To the international traveler, one of the most noticeable differences between North American and European cultures compared to African, Asian, and Australian cultures, is the collective consciousness of time in terms of how it is organized and influences lifestyles. In Eastern and Southern cultures, the pace of life is slower. People take their time going places and time is valued more than economic possibilities. Westerners, on the other hand, run wild from activity to activity, aggressively pursuing more. Economic possibility is valued more than the time or crafting it takes to achieve that potential.

Am I saying other cultures have no interest in earning money? Not at all. But, in other cultures, earnings do not define the self-worth of a person. Instead, intrinsic human value is found in what they do with their *time* rather than what they do with their *money*.

Before we look at some practical tips for adjusting a dollar-driven mindset to one that is more time-sensitive, let's look at how time and money related and were understood in biblical times.

Less feasting

What would the biblical landscape look like if our "time is money" perspective was present in the life of the ancient Hebrews and the early church?

First, there would have been fewer feasts and special celebrations. The Hebrews were commanded to rest one day out of every seven (see Exodus 35:2; Leviticus 23:3) and "rest" was more than just kicking off their sandals and taking a nap under a fig tree. Rest included gathering in sacred assembly to, as a people, remember and honor God (Leviticus 23:3).

These festivals and Sabbaths were the firstfruits of their time – an offering to God. Setting aside time in this manner reduced the ability of the people to harvest. Yet, on those limited earnings, multiple tithes were paid. In modern terms, they were definitely not maximizing their economic potential. Their time potential was extremely organized, however, and that meant their spiritual potential could be realized all the more.

Interestingly, most of the feasts and festivals were aligned with work:

- The Passover was celebrated just before harvest time.

- Pentecost happened just after the corn harvest.

- The Feast of Tabernacles began after the fruit of the ground had been gathered.

So in one sense, these gatherings demonstrated healthy respect for the people's earning abilities. However, the goal was not maximum capacity – not 24/7 capacity. It was a six-day work week, with the understanding that spiritual capacity needed to be expanded also. Managing time more than money was the method by which both goals could be achieved. Managing time allowed people to grow in assets, in cash flow, and *in giving*. Thus, the day of rest was established as a day of religious festivity and no working. As Jesus reminded the Pharisees, "the Sabbath was made for man, not man for the Sabbath" (Mark 2:27). Time during the Sabbath was to be devoted to three purposes: celebrating and worshipping God, working the land, and acting charitably.

> *Time ... was to be devoted to three purposes: celebrating and worshipping God, working the land, and acting charitably.*

Less sharing of power

So, if a "time is money" perspective had been in vogue during biblical times, there would have been fewer festivals. But, that's not the only aspect that would have changed. Under a "time is money" perspective, Moses may have been the first victim of "burnout."

When Jethro advised his son-in-law, Moses, to scale back and reassign some of his magisterial duties to others, he did so not to enable Moses to accumulate more things – more power, more accolades, more wealth. Jethro's recommendation came with a focus on the dispersion of authority and power. By incorporating delegation, Jethro saw three benefits: Moses would be able to stand the daily strain of his work, the people would be satisfied, and other leaders would be developed (Exodus 18:23).

According to Jethro, time was more valuable than control or power. But Jethro's advice was not only about delegation – he was also talking about excellence. He warned Moses, and the people, that they would wear out quickly at their current pace (v. 18). In delegating authority, Moses also dispersed the false idea that doing a lot of "things" honors God. Doing the tasks you're gifted for well – as opposed to doing many tasks in a mediocre manner – is what truly glorifies God (Colossians 3:23).

We see this again in Acts 6, when a food fight threatened to disrupt the burgeoning church. The apostles were, rightly, trying to focus on the ministry of the word and prayer, but there were disagreements between various factions over whether the widows were being properly cared for. It was a critical juncture for the apostles in terms of time and productivity. They could temporarily set aside the important ministry of teaching the Scriptures and devoting substantial time to prayer in order to hear the situation and discern a compassionate solution – or they could turn a deaf ear to the widows' arguments. *Or,* they could look for a better alternative. Thankfully, for the church then and for the church now, they chose to think a little differently. The apostles appointed those among them of high character and reputation to handle the situation. They delegated. And their actions remain an example to us today of how to lead in church, family, and workplace situations.

It was a classic example of "less is more." Many of us take on more things under the false assumption that more activity means more productivity, more life experiences, more respect, or more money to spend on more things. But Acts 6 demonstrates that doing less can bring more. Not only was food rationing expanded to include more widows, but the entire assembly was pleased the apostles stayed true to their call (Acts 6:5a). Most importantly, the gospel of Jesus was spread to more people (v. 7).

Group questions

1. *What services do you purchase to have more free time?*

2. *What things do you do yourself so you don't have to spend money to have others do them?*

3. *Review Exodus 18 and Acts 6. What else do you notice that could be added to this chapter's insights?*

4. *Identify a time for you when doing less helped you get more done.*

Example one: Deciding on the money

A married couple is considering the purchase of a used boat in excellent condition priced at $10,000. An accompanying trailer is $1,500 and an annual license is $125. Unfortunately, the motor is priced separately at $4,000. Fortunately, they already have a garage to hold it and a van to pull it. **Grand total:** $15,625, plus gasoline and unforeseen repairs (there are always unforeseen repairs). The family consults their bank account and discovers they can pay cash for half the cost. The other half they will need to finance over four years at 10 percent. **New grand total *with interest:*** somewhere north of $19,000, plus gasoline and those unforeseen repair bills. They believe they can afford the $330 monthly payment and soon they own a boat. This is deciding to purchase using money as the valuator – and it is the way most Western people approach purchases.

Example two: Deciding on the time

Another couple is considering buying the same boat. They too can only pay half down and would need to finance the remainder over four years. They look at the total $19,000 cost and break it down according to time. Between them they earn $41,000 per year. The husband currently has a half-time job, while the wife works full-time. The 300 working days they spend each year means they earn $137 a day, after taxes. A $19,000 boat purchase means they would need 136 working days to cover the cost of the boat. That is more than six months. Somehow, working six months to use a boat eight to 10 days a year loses its appeal and they decide not to buy. They are better off renting the boat from the first couple!

Time decisions have both short- and long-term consequences. When time value is driven by economics, a person gets trapped in a shortsighted view of life. They want more and they want it instantly. Every desire must be fulfilled without waiting. However, when economic cost is compared against time value, a long-term perspective emerges that allows us to consider the impact of decisions on something bigger and more important to God than our wallet: other people.

An emerging example of this is the growing popularity of stewardship investing. Stewardship investing is investing motivated and informed by one's faith convictions. The idea was born out of a desire to see money impact a greater good than simply one's pension fund. For example, suppose a multi-billion dollar oil company is dumping toxic waste into the ocean. The short-term, economics-driven viewpoint says, "No matter. Their stock has risen by 23 percent this year. I've made thousands of dollars."

However, the long-term, time-value approach says, "Over time, they will kill off many species of ocean life and pollute the rain and seas. What value (in time) is there if my children or I cannot swim in the ocean or eat the vegetables in my garden that were watered by polluted rain?" Time is profoundly connected to money, and understanding how and why can deepen our perspective.

Less eternal perspective

Finally, if the "time is money" approach had been lived out in the Bible, the focus on eternity would have been minimized. As it stands, there are thousands of references to eternity or eternal things in Scripture. There was a deep understanding among the early church that life in Christ exists far beyond the space and time of life on earth. This view of eternity should drive our decisions even today.

Paul reminds us that the wages of sin are death, but God's gift to us? Eternal life (Romans 6:23). Yes, Jesus came to give us abundant life, however this abundance was not in material things, but in Spirit (John 10:10). Scripture points out that everything that happens here on earth, while of utmost significance before God, is nonetheless passing. We are citizens of heaven first (Philippians 3:20). You may be a citizen of Italy, Brazil, the United States, or Puerto Rico, but if you call Christ your Lord, your true citizenship is established in God's realm, not in any kind of earthly kingdom.

This perspective should have a huge influence on money and time decisions. In Paul's first letter to Timothy, he wrote that temporal pursuits of money lead only to ruin (1 Timothy 6:10). Instead, Paul urged, "take hold of the eternal life to which you were called" (v. 12). As strange as it sounds, eternal life – something you cannot see, touch, or control – is the only thing you can truly hold on to. No matter how much you accumulate along the way, no U-Haul comes with your final earthly breath (v. 7).

As a result, money and time decisions made during this life need to embrace the eternity to which we are called. The result is a new paradigm – God's paradigm – that views money and time in terms of how they are used *together* to benefit others. This eternal perspective on money and time shifts the focus from "what's in it for me?" to "what's in it for others and their eternity?"

I am not going to be in heaven by myself. There will be a countless multitude. But the decisions I make in regard to time and money today can influence heaven's roll call. As Randy Alcorn has said, "The money we give to help others on earth will open doors of fellowship with them in heaven."[3]

Thoughts from the wealthy

Comments from the world's wealthiest people at the end of their lives make a fascinating study. They all arrived at the same conclusion: time is not about money.

John Rockefeller: "I know of nothing more despicable and pathetic than a man who devotes all the hours of the waking day to the making of money for money's sake."[4] (Rockefeller considered money, and the ability to make it, a gift of God to be shared.)

King Solomon: His earthly riches had never been equaled before, but Solomon surmised that it was all meaningless. "Now all has been heard; here is the conclusion of the matter: Fear God and keep his commandments, for this is the whole duty of man (Ecclesiastes 12:13)." The temporal did not satisfy. The eternal was more than satisfying.

King David: Israel's mighty king lamented that, "We are merely moving shadows, and all our busy rushing ends in nothing (Psalm 39:6). Everything we accumulate gets passed on to someone else. "Our only hope is in God," he concluded (v. 7).

Remember Benjamin Franklin's quote at the beginning of this chapter? *"…time is money. Money can beget money, and its offspring can beget more. The way to wealth is … waste neither time nor money."* There is wisdom in that quote. It is true that you must spend time to earn money, but that doesn't automatically equate an intrinsic value. You could spend $5 on a stuffed animal, but the value of your gift is not $5 – the value of your gift is the joy it brings to a child's face. The value is the feeling in your heart of helping other people feel better about themselves, the world around them, and their intrinsic value before God. In the end, time is the most precious of commodities – not money.

Starting points

1. **The power of compound interest.** Compound interest is at work even when you are not. When you eat lunch, go to sleep, or go on vacation, the numbers are still turning over. A reminder that "investments don't collect dust when I'm not working" can be a calming reminder. But remember, debt makes compound interest work in reverse! Debts, too, grow on days you don't work, and this knowledge can add to your anxiety and level of stress. It can also force you to consume your time in ways that do not reflect spiritual priorities.

2. **Consider the power of compound interest in eternal terms.** I may have $10,000 in principal, but another $4,000 in interest over time was generated by exponential mathematics – not by me. What if that interest could be reinvested in the underprivileged and underserved? Mother Teresa once said, "God did not create poverty. Man did when he refused to share."

3. **Organize your daily life around time, not money.** Consider the following possibility: A restaurant manager decides to do things differently than the rest of the restaurants in her chain. Rather than measuring how much money she could generate per seating, she begins focusing on generating repeat business with people who devote an entire evening to dining. Now she seats fewer people during the prime time, but generates more revenue per customer as a result. Servers receive larger tips, too. And, the restaurant is now busier during the afternoon, with business people scheduling meetings with clients during the usually slower period. Now she has long-term relationships with her customers. She is closer to them and their ever-changing tastes.

4. **Re-establish Sabbath in your life.** Try saying these words: Worship. Naps. Unstructured time. Learn to like how those words sound coming out of your mouth.

Prayer:

Lord, as we look at the relationship between time and money, we know that we're going to see some connections that will challenge us. Help us to see what you see in these discussions, and help us to want what you want. Be with our decisions about how to spend both our time and our money, and remind us to keep an eternal perspective in mind.

Amen.

End questions

1. Most North Americans set aside two days each week – Saturday and Sunday – to rest from weekly toil. So, why don't we feel more rested – physically or spiritually?

2. How often do you think about your time and money decisions from a "here and now" perspective? How often from an eternal perspective? Share examples.

3. If an inventory of how you spend time were made, it would clearly show that the most important thing in your life is: _____ (fill in the blank). What does that say to you?

4. How do we break free from the cultural snares that constantly call for more and more?

Sources

1   Much of the material used in this chapter came from "Time Warped: First Century Time Stewardship for 21st Century Living," by Steve Ganger, MMA, 2004.

2   Selections from Benjamin Franklin's letter, *Advice to a Young Tradesman*, 1748.

3   Alcorn, Randy. "The Treasure Principle." Sisters, OR: Multnomah (1997), 38.

4   Quoted in Lewis H. Lapham, "Money and Class in America," note to Chapter 8 (1988).

Money and Stress

Money pressures, debt, and unwise decisions can add to stress. As can unexpected medical expenses or the need to provide assistance to aging parents. An employee steals from you and the stealing impacts your current and future income due to fallout with customers. Your father dies, and the loss is multiplied by the stress of selling some of his things and moving your mother into an apartment. A stroke means your mom can't care for herself, and you are the only family nearby. Your annual property tax assessment went up – again. You receive the new schedule of school fees for your children's education. Stress. Stress. Stress.

When thinking about money and stress, let's start with Hans Selye. Selye was a Swedish researcher who studied how stressful situations affected people. He noted stress could affect health and the ability for the body to heal itself. But his main findings were that stress reactions are individual and variable. One person gets hives or itchy scalp. Another gets painful canker sores. Still another gets loose bowels, or an upset stomach, or gains weight from eating comfort foods. Do any of these sound familiar?

Headaches and back pain are also possible stress responses, but everyone's reactions to stress are different. What stresses some people is not stressful to others, and whenever stress is experienced, it plays out in our bodies in different ways.

> *Physiological reactions to stress include increased: Heart rate, blood pressure, breathing rate, use of energy, muscle tension.*

It's important to realize that the standard stress response is the same thing as the fight-or-flight response. There is a set of physiological reactions that occur when we perceive a situation as threatening, dangerous, or out of our control. Our bodies respond, ready to fight or flee, to get us away from what we perceive as dangerous. But in modern society, we rarely do either. We remain on our couch, or seated at our desk, or we continue driving in our car. This means the energy released in our body to fight or run goes somewhere else.

When the brain senses a stressful situation, it tells the body to release specific hormones that help you get into action quicker to run away from or fight the cause of your stress. These responses include everything from an increased heart rate, higher blood pressure, increased metabolism, and tension in the muscles. These reactions are complex and affect other systems in your body. If the stress is unrelenting, and the response is elicited frequently and over a prolonged period of time, the effects may have harmful long-term consequences. Some of those long-term effects could include decreased energy, high blood pressure, depression, psychiatric disorders, frequent infections, exhaustion, heart disease, headaches, and, possibly, certain types of cancers.

Money dynamics and stress

Money dynamics add to stress. Imagine for a moment that the elderly parents of four Christian siblings have died, and the children have gathered to divide what little estate their parents had. There are petty snipings and unkind behaviors all around. Grief mingles with greed as they compete to possess trinkets that trigger memories of their childhood. The two sons fight over their father's tie clip or cufflinks. The sisters become alienated for years because one takes for herself "mother's ring" that the other felt she should have received. Death was bad enough. Money issues make it worse. Somewhere along the way, they forget about their commitments to Jesus – and to living out their faith.

Money consumes so much of our lives. Earning it. Spending it. Saving it. Filling all our troubled moments every bit as much as it fills our successes. A woman has a tumor checked, believing it is cancerous. The resulting surgery eats up all her budgeted medical expenses for the year. In situations like these, where we must manage a crisis and money is involved, we might not even think about being a Christian. We just react. Our faith might come through and have influence some of the time, but it certainly does not come from conscious planning.

And it is not just whether faith shines through when there is stress and money involved. It is also a question of how you treat other people and how you take care of yourself physically and emotionally (or don't). Money and its accompanying stresses are pervasive. If your faith isn't as deeply ingrained as your love of money, then more trouble – more stress – will come.

Money and its accompanying stresses are pervasive. If your faith isn't as deeply ingrained as your love of money, then more trouble – more stress – will come.

Some of the additional stress is obvious, but some of it is subtle. You can trace some stress to your choices, but other stress comes from choices others make that effect you. Money dynamics can add to the intensity.

Sometimes when there is stress, we remind ourselves that we shouldn't complain. We should keep it all in perspective and calm down. Our bills are paid, we tell ourselves. Or we remind our children that we have more than we need. We might even compare ourselves to someone we consider less fortunate, so that our stress is somehow diminished.

And it might be somewhat comforting to do this – but only to a point. Anxiety is anxiety. Stress is stress. Why would stress be different for you just because you have money and others do not? In fact, you might have even more stress as a person of some economic comfort than a person who has nothing but a hut and the open sky.

Money-related stress

Money can cause stress, directly or indirectly.

Direct effect of money on stress: Your phone bill is due, and you don't have money to cover it. If the bill isn't paid in full, your phone service will be turned off, so you become frustrated and anxious because you need phone service for your work. You are also stressed about the unpaid bill and the fees that will accumulate monthly. The stress you are experiencing is a direct result of the lack of money to pay the bill.

Indirect effect of money on stress: You promised your daughter a special 16th birthday party. She has planned for months to invite several friends to dinner at a restaurant and a movie afterwards. A week before the party, an unanticipated bill leaves no money for the party. Your daughter is disappointed and angry. She thinks you've cheated her and her friends. She cries and won't talk to you for several days.

You become upset and sad over disappointing your daughter. Plus, you feel incompetent and embarrassed in front of your daughter and her friends for having miscalculated so badly. Your stress is a response to the disappointment your daughter experienced, rather than the direct result of the shortage of money. You may not have been bothered at all about not having enough money for the party, but your daughter's response, and the way it affects your relationship with her, causes you stress.

Let's look again at the woman who is worried about her tumor and has a lumpectomy. There is stress because she has to have surgery. There is additional stress because she has to take a week off work, and she's already used up her sick time for this year. Because she is a wife and mother, she also feels conflicted because family resources are being used on her, and that takes away from what she wants to give to her family. Perhaps she feels guilty that she has health insurance when her neighbor does not.

People without resources seldom carry the stress of guilt those who *do* have resources carry. Many Western people experience stress over having – and then not having. Additional economic options give them additional reasons to be stressed. In some ways, people in poverty experiences stress more intensely, but their list of things that cause stress is shorter.

A person without means has no car, but a person with a car experiences stress if he blows a tire in heavy traffic. People without obligations have no appointments, but a person with responsibilities feels stress if she is running late. A poor person does not have much food, but a person with money may experience stress if a pizza delivery is late.

Group questions

1. Have you experienced any of the symptoms of stress referred to earlier? Can you link them back to a specific time of stress? Was there any connection to money?

2. Return to the theme text of this book (2 Corinthians 8:1-7, especially verse 5). How do you think money stress might have affected the Macedonian Christians? Do you think there is an adverse connection between money stress and generosity? If so, why?

3. Are there links between your stress and your economic means? How might you experience stress differently if you possessed fewer things or took on fewer responsibilities?

4. Read 1 Peter 5: 6-11. Focus especially on verse 7. How might this advice assist a person who is experiencing stress?

Effects of stress

Physically	Emotionally	Spiritually
• Increased heart rate.	• Relationships with family members are always affected. Marriages suffer from the stress of financial disagreements or difficulties.	• Financial difficulties can make it hard to be honest with God or communicate with God. Relationships with people in the church, and with God, are affected negatively or are compromised.
• Increased respiration.		
• Increased blood pressure, eventual high blood pressure, and/or heart disease.		
• Exhaustion.	• Children sense their parents' stress. Parents become impatient and irritable. Your ability to cope with normal frustrations decreases.	
• Stomach problems, indigestion, and changes in appetite.		• Reading Scripture becomes difficult.
• Decreased resistance to illness.		• Stress makes it difficult to focus our prayers.
• Muscle aches and headaches.	• Other relationships become strained and uncomfortable. Some people may become less open and less willing to communicate.	• Stress takes time and time is what God demands.
• Poor nutrition and/or overweight or underweight.		
• Possibly some types of cancer.	• Prolonged biochemical changes increase the chances for clinical depression and other emotional disorders.	

Coping

Some people sleep when they are stressed. Others engage in frenetic activity. Still others eat a lot – or stop eating. Some lash out; others pull back. A Christian needs to respond in peace, not in panic. Remember, stress is variable and individual. It is not the event happening to you that causes the stress, but rather your perception of and reaction to the event. We all have control over some of our responses to stress.

Sometimes it may seem you have little control over events. It is true that there are circumstances over which we have no control. It is also true that some situations grant us a good deal of control. It is important to accurately identify those situations where you have control and those where you do not. Then you can prioritize your responses.

When money is connected to stress, it is important to identify what the financial issues are. Doing so is a significant step in decreasing stress.

> *When money is connected to stress, it is important to identify what the financial issues are.*

In order to decrease stress, you have to know and understand what your relationship with money is. Discovering and detailing this relationship requires time. All other strategies to cope with stress are secondary if your relationship with money is not clearly understood. Once accomplished, the goal is to address the issues where you have control and adjust your reactions to issues over which you have no control.

Here are some broad-based strategies:

• Clarify your relationship with money and what money means to you as a Christian.

• Adjust your priorities and goals to fit this description.

• For those priorities and goals that cannot be adjusted, identify strategies to manage the effects of stress.

Here are some more comprehensive approaches:

1. Define and clarify your relationship with money and its role in your life. If this relationship isn't clearly defined, there will be frustration. Part of the definition centers on what place God plays in your relationship with money. You must be conscious of this relationship or other activities suggested here will not be effective.

2. Develop financial goals, priorities, and plans based on your relationship with money as defined above (revisit Chapter 1 if needed). Using goals as your guide, determine how money helps you achieve these goals. Be realistic. Build flexibility into your plan. Life changes. Flexibility is key to getting through those changes.

3. Set clear limits and avoid temptations. Establishing clear financial limits on spending and consuming helps. Avoid opportunities to spend money. Don't go places where you will be tempted to spend. Don't look at advertisements, magazines, or catalogs – and going to sales is no excuse – you will only spend more to save a little.

4. Communication and compromise are key to working out these issues. Your own thoughts, goals, and priorities must be communicated to your spouse (if married), your children (at age-appropriate levels), and perhaps, your parents, siblings, or church group. If there are significant differences to overcome, you will need to cooperate to bring goals and priorities together. No one gets everything. Healthy relationships require healthy communication and commitment. The only communication and commitment you have control over, however, is your own.

5. Seek professional help. There are qualified people available if more extensive help is needed. Don't overlook your pastoral staff.

6. Pray. Find times and places to de-stress from life's financial pressures. Turn everything off, including cell phones, telephones, laptops, personal stereos – all of it. It's easy to become unfocused with many distractions and temptations surrounding you. It is worth the time and effort to get away and regroup.

7. If you cannot avoid financial stress, find ways to manage it. Here are some suggestions:

- Breathe in slowly and deeply through your nose, count to four, exhale slowly counting to four. Do this 5-10 times.

- With your eyes closed, tense your muscles. Hold a few seconds. Beginning at your feet, focus on relaxing your muscle groups as you gradually progress up your body to your head. Stay that way for a full minute before opening your eyes.

- Pause and count to 10 very slowly. This helps you gain perspective and relax.

- If what you're doing is causing the stress, take a break, and come back later. This can lessen stress and when you return, you may be less affected.

- Exercise is among the most significant ways to reduce stress. Walking briskly, running, biking fast, or some other active sport, helps expend built-up energy and frustration caused by financial stress. Exercise also decreases tension and clears your mind.

- As in all of life, God is your guide and help. These issues are too tough to handle alone. God is always there – share with him your concerns, fears, and stress in prayer. Ask for strength and guidance. Then, thank him and leave the things causing you stress with him.

Prayer:

*Lord, money – and the stress it can bring – can rule our lives if
we don't take care to keep you first. Help us to remember what stress is
and how to combat it. Help us, Lord, also to use stress to our advantage
when that is appropriate. As Christians, we want to always respond in peace,
not in panic. Help us turn to you at these moments and remember, always,
where our hope lies. Bless you, God, and be with us, we pray.*

Amen.

End questions

1. When you are under stress, what is your typical response? How can you modify that response based on what you learned in this chapter?

2. Can too much money be as stressful as too little? If yes, in what ways?

3. Have you learned to be content in all things, as the Apostle Paul was? If not, in which areas of your life does contentment elude you? Can you think of ways to address this?

Special thanks to Kelli Burkholder King, MMA's health and wellness consultant, for this chapter's contents.

One other resource that may be helpful is the book "A Christian View of Money: Celebrating God's Generosity," by Mark L. Vincent, Herald Press, 1997. This book is available from MMA.

The Sandwich Generation

Different time periods and changing cultures have changed the look of the basic family unit. In ancient times, people lived several generations in the same small house or tent. Abraham, his wife Sarah, his father Terah, and his nephew Lot formed a household (Genesis 11-13). Later the household included a surrogate mother Hagar, the son Ishmael whom she had with Abraham, and later, Isaac, once Sarah finally conceived.

Economic survival throughout history, and in most of the world today, means extended families pool their resources in order to eat and have shelter and medical care. Only in the wealthiest societies have nuclear families (parents and their children) and now single-adult households become a societal norm. Compare this with an immigrant community in central Los Angeles that has three families in a house, all of them pooling resources to make a house payment and cover the one car they share between them.

In contemporary wealthy societies, there are many derivations on what defines a family. Some people live together without getting married – then go on their way once love cools. Others stay together, though, and have children, but still without getting married. Others enter into new relationships and have children with their new mate before the divorce from their previous mate is final. And now we are into societal debate about homosexual marriage, genetic manipulation of children, and who bears financial responsibility for the care of aging parents.

Perhaps, in the middle of all this mess, it is wise to return to the beginning – thinking again about what constitutes a family and *then* try to make sense of it all. In so doing, we will discover that current forms of family are not economically sustainable and that multi-generation households are in the best position to weather economic turmoil.

> *Current forms of family are not economically sustainable.*

Group questions

1. Map out the family relationships in the following Scripture passages: Genesis 46:1-7; Ruth 1:14-22 and 4:13-15; Acts 4:32-37; 1 Timothy 5:1-4. What are your observations about the makeup of these families?

2. What types of families exist in your extended network? What percentage of families today would you guess live in a multi-generation household?

3. Are the numbers of multi-generation families increasing or decreasing in your experience? Why?

Household history

Prior to 1940, the average family included parents from intact households, usually living close to, if not on the same farm, as their own parents. The children of those parents didn't move far away either. Western society and economy was primarily agricultural.

In the years of World War II and following, the family shifted a bit. Now, when people left their birth families to form their own families, they *really left*. The apron strings were cut, so to speak. Moving from the farm to urban industrial employment, many people no longer lived anywhere near their families of origin. This means they established fully independent households.

Often, children lived far away from their parents as they pursued education, worked, or raised families of their own. While grandparents were disappointed to have their children living so far away, *their* children raised their families with the assumption their offspring would live elsewhere. It wasn't that they minded having them close by – they just didn't think it would happen.

Think about what that meant economically. Before 1940, people lived as multiple generations in the same house or at least on the same land. They pooled their resources. Many children did not have independent income until they married. But since 1970, many families – and many individuals – have independent incomes and they are trying to cover the same expenses that three generations living together had to cover previously.

Consider this example: A couple divorces and the former wife and the children return to her family of origin. They pool resources as an extended family to do whatever it takes to put a life together for everyone. The former husband is alienated from his family of origin and must cover all of his expenses. In this scenario, even if the former husband earns more income, the former wife is economically more secure.

To reach this understanding, one must count economic resources as something more than mere income. Reduced expenses, multiple uses of an asset, and shared labor are economic benefits a lone individual doesn't have.

> *One must count economic resources as something more than mere income.*

This is often where someone raises the objection about family members who mooch off those who are more secure economically. And while it is a certainty that some family members do not or cannot play their part, taking more than they give, this dynamic is also present in the marketplace. Whether one lives among several generations or lives alone, one cannot escape the dynamic of those willing to absorb all the handouts that come their way.

Did you know some economists call children an expense – a liability on the family fortunes? They do so because society seems to have stopped counting the economic benefits of secure and covenantal relationships.

The point is, paying for everything yourself at all times is difficult, especially when you arrive at a point in life when you need people to care for you. People who live alone and who run from secure relationships seldom have friends and family who surround a hospital bedside. Those friends and family who do come, look more like carrion than support.

As the world moved on, many children who grew up and lived separate from their parents did not remain married – if, indeed, they married at all. Couples were together for a time, had children, then set up separate households, perhaps with another partner, perhaps not. Thus, their children came from homes without two parents and repeated the pattern – again perhaps marrying, perhaps not – their children often moving far away and everyone trying to make ends meet on independent incomes. A new trend begins to emerge: childbearing with or without a partner, and with or without a family. The trend continues and the problem worsens.

What will happen if we keep going in this direction instead of returning to multi-generation households? Well, look for a continuing high divorce rate among those who marry. *Their* children will continue to live far away, often not bothering to create a household with someone, but having children nonetheless. Their children are likely to do the same. In other words, without some major changes, either by choice or by tragedy, individuals will keep trying to pay for ever more pricey lifestyles from an ever more selfish basis – and then, tragically, find it economically devastating. But even worse, at life's end, they will be alone.

In my family, we have recently learned more about the principles of community living than we would have ever imagined. Allow me to share with you an excerpt from my newsletter, Depth Perception, from April 15, 2002 (Depth Perception is available from www.DesignForMinistry.com):

"My wife's battle with cancer is now well into its third year. During this difficult period we have been victim to more generosity than we've ever been able to commit in both our lifetimes. Whether it was a monetary gift, being surrounded in a circle of prayer, a sincere 'how are you doing,' a bouquet of sugar cookies baked into floral shapes, a timely phone call, or the many e-mails we call e-ncouragements, we've learned to count ourselves among the most fortunate of people.

"Judaism teaches the principle of tzedakah (righteousness/justice). In his book "The Kabbalah of Money," Rabbi Nilton Bonder describes engaging in tzedakah as participation in the celestial economy. For example, by being a business person who charges a fair price and demonstrates excellent customer service as a matter of integrity, I not only do a good business here on earth, I store up assets of goodwill and grace in God's account – grace I might need to draw on in a time of crisis. Having been married to Lorie for nearly 18 years, I am qualified to testify that this is the manner in which she lives. During our time of need we received vast withdrawals from her stores.

"Our experience leads us to mourn for those who do not have a community of family or friends such as ours. Perhaps they are victims of incredible cruelty, or perhaps it is a lifestyle choice that leaves them bereft at the inauguration of suffering. So many are abandoned at the time of their greatest need. So many are treated with prejudice or callousness so that physical illness becomes but one item on their long and continuing list of anguish.

"Living with cancer is unimaginably hard. Every case is unique because of the person, their family systems, and their unique set of choices and experiences that come with them. Everyone who faces it is in a unique territory that no one else can fully perceive. How awful it must be to enter that territory with no traveling companions, multiplying and far reaching concerns, and the echo of rejection as loved ones walk away!

"Jesus tells us that those of us who mourn will be comforted. Whether we mourn our disease or the dis-ease of others and the additional suffering they inflict on us, this is a wonderful promise to know. What we must realize is that this comfort often happens at the hand of others, and that their ability to comfort us exists in proportion to our having lived others-centered lives from the beginning."

Group questions

1. *What reactions do you have to these observations about the linkage of family relationships and economic well being?*

2. *What sort of family did you come from? How does that fact impact your own family today?*

Observations about change

Do you want to be part of a trend that turns us from this extreme form of individualism? Would you like to see Western families living more economically sustainable lives? Would you like a return to mutual aid, neighborliness, and trusting relationships?

First, it is important to know that money flows in the direction the family goes. If the family stays together, family economic assets benefit everyone. If the family divides along individual lines, everyone has only what they have and multiple uses of assets disappear.

> *Money flows in the direction the family goes.*

Those who live as divided or blended families might object and say they still share and assist each other. This is quite possible, but it is often a pressure, a hardship, a much greater sacrifice. It often isn't the family's priority – and they do it because they feel guilty rather than because it is natural to their commitments. The result is they share, perhaps, but far less and far less often than an extended family would.

Second, the choices that lead families to pursue individual directions are the same type of choices that lead people to mismanage money. They want what they want *right now*, regardless of the cost. The result is they intensify the money problems and the unsustainability of living so independently. They already have financial pressures from legal issues, child support payments, or trying to raise children on one income. Their spending habits and use of credit just make matters worse. And "worse" does not mean just the individual and their life with money. "Worse" includes all of society, because there is no longer a family support system to pay for medical care or the nursing home, or to care for children. People who make these choices end up without a supporting family and have little to no estate. The essence of their life is consumption of what a previous generation gave them, what they created through their own work, and any inheritance they might pass along to children and society at-large. Their population is growing, and they will vote for politicians who promise them government support when they become frail.

This is the key reason the current direction is unsustainable. Imagine the future demand if all multi-generation households come to an end and every individual spends a portion of his or her life in a nursing home before they die. Imagine that most of them cannot afford the cost of a nursing home. Add in an aging population that increases the number of people going through this pipeline and a large and tragic mess develops.

Does this sound like pessimism? It does not have to be. If people discover they cannot grow their income fast enough to keep up with the vast array of choices before them, they might begin to consolidate resources again. It might not look like the agricultural communities of pre-World War II, but perhaps out of sheer necessity they will live in multi-generation households and once again pool their economic resources.

I consider my own children. Because of my wife's health needs, we returned to Wisconsin and live near her sister. The result is a set of four adults who are significantly involved in the upbringing of the five children we share between us. Grandparents have spent significant time with us – as well as other family members and friends who are passing through. The pooling of our efforts on behalf of each other has made for a far less expensive life.

> *The pooling of our efforts on behalf of each other has made for a far less expensive life.*

A third observation of note is that few people have ever lived in what we identify as the traditional nuclear family: a mom, a dad, and 2.3 children in a suburban housing division, with manicured lawns and white picket fences. Many people lived this way recently, but it was a blip on the timeline and limited to Western culture. On a global level, the multi-generation household was, is, and likely will be where the majority of people will be raised – and where they will raise their families. We might not all live under the same roof at the same time, but we did and will think of family as a larger unit of generations, not just parent-child.

Here are three examples from Scripture. The first is Abraham. When he went to Canaan he brought his father and a nephew with him. He and Sarah agreed that their childlessness could end if they requested her handmaiden bear Abraham's child (a widespread practice to combat infertility in those days).

Another example is the Apostle Paul writing to the New Testament churches. When he describes how people were to act as Christians, he breaks it down according to the household of the day: older women should teach younger women; older men should teach younger men; and parents should teach children (Titus 2; Ephesians 5 and 6).

A third example is when Paul wrote to Timothy, talking about his mother and grandmother, and describing how both of them were involved in his spiritual heritage (2 Timothy 1:5).

I'd like to make one final observation: We can be hopeful about these problems. With a little work and a little planning, just about any family system can improve its economic sustainability. Those who remain pessimistic or defeated do so because they want quick solutions that result in perfect circumstances — without any planning or maintenance.

If you wonder what kind of planning is being referred to, take a moment to review the first two chapters of this book. Teach all the children in your life to distinguish between giving, saving, providing, and consuming. Make it a part of the discipleship classes your congregation offers. Embed it in pre-marital preparation. Expect it from those who come asking for financial assistance. Talk freely about your estate plan. Tell your children about your financial goals and your status in reaching them. Talk about your heritage and the heritage you intend to pass on. This is what the instruction to families in Deuteronomy 6 was all about:

"These words which I am commanding you today, shall be on your heart: and you shall teach them diligently to your children and shall talk of them when you sit in your house and when you walk by the way and when you lie down and when you rise up. And you shall bind them as a sign on your hand and they shall be as frontals on your forehead. And you shall write them on the doorposts of your house and on your gates" (Deuteronomy 6:4-9).

Prayer:

God, thank you for the strong examples of family provided in the Bible and for the blessing of our own extended families. Whether or not we live together in multi-generation situations, help us to recognize, again, the gift from you our family members are. Help us to treasure them and to treat them with the respect and honor due them as your gift to us. Open our eyes to ways we can consolidate the use of certain resources with our family members.

Amen.

End questions

1. *Does your family have a financial plan? Does this plan take into account issues of long-term care and the possibility of dependent family members?*

2. *Have you discussed money management with your children? Have they begun to manage money effectively?*

3. *What response will you have if your parent or an adult child suddenly needs your support? Is your home open? If married, would your spouse agree?*

4. *Are you prepared to give up your current home and live in a smaller space for the welfare of the family as a whole?*

Living on Enough

by Lynn Miller, Stewardship Theologian, MMA

*Lynn Miller, stewardship theologian at MMA, has dealt with this subject as
broadly as anyone I know. My calling to minister in the area of faith and
money grew out of his work. I was privileged to work with him at MMA.
In the years since, he has been an on-going source of encouragement.*

*Lynn's voice still resonates strongly in the two articles he wrote for this
book – as you will see when you read this chapter and the next. I encourage
you to take the time to jot down your thoughts. When you have finished
reading these chapters, consider discussing your thoughts with other members
of your household or a close friend.*

– Mark

When I was in college, I remember learning what were called the Immutable
Laws of the Universe. Laws like "Whatever goes up must come down" (Law of
Gravity) and "Everything, given enough time, falls apart" (Second Law of
Thermodynamics).

Every afternoon when I left the campus and got back into the real world of
paying rent and buying groceries for my growing family, I discovered a third
immutable law – the Law of Need Versus Money. This law says that the amount of
money that will be enough to live on will always be more than the amount of
money I have. Maybe you can relate?

Interestingly, over the last 40 years, I saw the Law of Gravity broken by the
space program, and the Second Law of Thermodynamics confirmed by politics.
But for a long time in my life, the Law of Need Versus Money remained firmly in
place. No matter how much money I made, it was never enough. When I was in
voluntary service in 1971, our family of four received a grand total of $30 a
month cash – plus groceries and rent. Obviously *that* was never enough. You
can't clothe and educate two growing children on $30 a month.

But one year later, when I was making $8.88 an hour as a journeyman car-
penter in California, it still wasn't enough. And I soon came to the conclusion
that no matter how much money I made, it wouldn't be enough. At this point in

the Great War Against My Own Poverty, I began looking for a place to surrender. I gave up. I decided I was not going to spend my life fighting a losing battle between my needs and my money.

But, surrendering didn't solve the problem either. I wasn't fighting the battle anymore, but I was still losing the war. No matter how much I trimmed my needs, I still needed more. And no matter how much I increased my income, I still needed more.

> *I wasn't fighting the battle anymore, but I was still losing the war.*

Then I stumbled across another immutable law of the universe, this one from the Bible. In his letter to the Philippians, Paul wrote that he had learned to be content with whatever he had. He learned the secret of being content in every situation, whether well fed or hungry, having plenty or being in need. And the secret, Paul says, is knowing that you can do "all things through Christ who strengthens him (Philippians 4:12-13)." This is what I call the Law of the Meaning of Stuff. This law has two parts.

Part 1: Everything has meaning

That everything has some meaning is pretty obvious. Cars, for example, can mean transportation, convenience, pleasure, status, or any number of other values. Houses can mean shelter, hospitality, prestige, expense, or investment. Food can mean nutrition, pleasure, comfort, or hospitality – and so on.

Of course, money also has various meanings (power, status, generosity), but once you start looking at what your stuff means, you soon begin to see that some meanings work *for* you and some work *against* you.

If you think the type of car you drive indicates your importance as a person, what do you do when someone else buys a more luxurious or prestigious car? If you believe the size or style of your house means you are a person of good taste and prestige, what happens when someone down the street builds a bigger or more luxurious house? And if the meaning you attach to your salary is that you are a person well thought of by your company, what happens when someone else at the company gets a bigger salary than you? Do you see the problem? You can never get enough "stuff" to fulfill some of your meanings. But the answer to that problem is found in the second part of the law.

Part 2: *What something means is up to you*

Good news: *You choose what your stuff means.* You can either "buy" the mean-ing advertisers are trying to sell you, or you can decide for yourself what meaning you will attach to your things. For example, if you decide your house means shelter instead of prestige, then how big it needs to be depends on how much shelter you need – not on how big your neighbor's house is. If you decide your car means transportation instead of status, then the kind of car you buy is driven by what kind of transportation you need – not what the world thinks about you. And if you decide your money is just a means of exchange you use to fulfill your other needs, then you only need enough money to do that.

When I discovered I could choose the meanings I attached to my stuff, I real-ized I was finally getting somewhere in the Great War Against My Own Poverty. I needed money, but only enough to buy what I needed. I needed food, but only enough to remain healthy. I needed a car, but only the kind of car that would give me reliable transportation. I needed a house to live in, but only the kind and size of house that would fulfill my need for shelter. My needs for comfort, ego stroking, and prestige could be met elsewhere.

But where? Where would I fulfill these needs to feel good about myself – to feel loved and appreciated? Remember Paul's secret to contentment? "I can do all things through Christ who strengthens me." That is where true fulfillment comes from: Jesus Christ.

Wow, what a source! Now that I think of it, no amount of "stuff" could give me the love and status I get from having the one sinless man in history give his life for mine. Nothing I can buy can do that – only the free gift of salvation in and from Jesus Christ (Romans 5:15-17).

But that means my Law of the Meaning of Stuff comes with a warning: If only the free gift of the life, death, and resurrection of Jesus Christ can give you this kind of love, then putting money in Jesus' place is not going to work. Money only falls into place if you put Jesus first as the head of your life.

Then, living on enough becomes easier, because "enough" is defined by the inherent usefulness of the product, whatever it is, instead of what the advertiser says about it. Notice that living on enough does not equal doing without. It means making clear calculations about what is enough for you – outside of the influence of advertising designed to sell, sell, sell more product. Completing those calculations may be the greatest blessing you ever receive. Nothing is more fun, or liberating, than walking through a shopping mall and realizing you don't need any of the stuff they have for sale! And few things are more satisfying than looking at your paycheck and thanking God you are receiving more than you need – and therefore a raise in pay only means you have the ability to give or save even more.

Group questions

1. In what ways have you experienced the Law of Need Versus Money in your life? How have you either given in to this law or fought it?

2. In Philippians 4:12-13, Paul writes about learning to be content in all things. In which areas of your life do you struggle with being content? How might you begin to win those struggles?

3. In contemporary society, is it possible to remain free of the materialistic manipulations of our media-saturated world? If not, how can you combat these manipulations without moving to a secluded mountaintop in Tibet?

Living on enough and using credit

Most budget courses discourage the use of credit. Some even suggest debt should be avoided at all costs. But completely avoiding debt can lead to a feeling of deprivation – and can cost more in the long run than using debt wisely. Debt is a tool. It is, in itself, neither good nor evil.

> *Completely avoiding debt can lead to a feeling of deprivation – and can cost more in the long run.*

When I built my home, I had to break up some existing concrete to put in the sewer line. So I rented a jackhammer. If I had used that jackhammer for a whole week, I could have bought it cheaper than renting it. But I only needed the jackhammer for a few hours, so I rented it.

A house mortgage or an automobile loan is kind of like that – only you're renting money instead of a jackhammer. You don't need to have all the money it takes to buy a house or a car, you only need the money for a short time: 30 years (or so) for a home, two years for a used car. So you "rent" the money you need to buy the home or the car, and pay it back in monthly installments. Another way to look at a house mortgage is that the interest payment is what you would have paid to rent an apartment or house, and the principle is a form of savings. Plus, for free, you get the appreciation on the home while you live in it and own it.

In these examples, we're talking about buying something that either increases wealth or produces income. In the case of a house, you can live in it and add value to it by working on it. The problem with consumer debt is borrowing money to buy things that have *no* potential to increase in value or produce income. Instead of a house or a car, you're buying a dining experience, your 27th shirt, or a 14th pair of shoes. Most people in credit card trouble get there by not knowing what they can afford – or what they really need. In fact, most people who overspend do so because they discover spending is fun! Shopping is *entertainment* in our culture. We even have a name for those who love to go shopping. Shopaholics. Now, getting a good deal is not only fun, it's addictive!

We learn what shopping means from our families and our culture. A recent Wal-Mart television advertisement makes the point. In the ad, a silver-haired couple is pushing a shopping cart down the aisle in the store while saying, "We come here four or five days a week and just enjoy seeing all the things we didn't know we needed!" Now that's good training for shopaholics!

Fortunately there is a cure – and that cure is to find one's sense of purpose and sense of worth in following Christ rather than Sam Walton.

In the industrial world, Americans are the worst at saving money, but we're the best at making loan payments. Think about that a minute. Making a savings deposit and making a loan payment are the exact same transaction. You fill out a slip of paper (deposit slip or payment slip), you write a check, you put it into an envelope, and you mail it or drop it off. The only difference is someone else is getting the money when you make a loan payment. You, however, get the money when you make a deposit. Changing who gets the money is easy.

Changing who gets the money is easy.

Want to make that loan payment go the other way? Here's what you do. When the loan is paid off, keep making the payments. But this time make them in the form of deposits to your savings or investment account. You have already learned the discipline of making the payment; now just change who gets the money. You'll be surprised at how much a loan payment is worth in the years to come.

Imagine you had a college loan that you paid off (at a rate of $400 a month) by the time you turned 30. In 35 years, when you reach retirement age, that same $400-a-month payment could add up to more than $1 million if you continued to invest it each month and received an average of 10 percent growth during those 35 years. But, even if you cannot save that entire $400 every month during those years, there would still be a substantial benefit to you if you saved as much of it as possible instead of purchasing more stuff you don't need, or a bigger house with more room than you'll use, or a luxury car that's more than simply reliable transportation. Of course, you'd have to actually pay off your loan before you could start paying yourself – and find ways to sidestep the temptation to keep up with your neighbors as they buy bigger and more luxurious homes, cars, whatever. But since you know that, for you, the inherent usefulness of these things has nothing to do with a level of luxury, you could avoid that expensive trap.

Prayer:

Lord, check my heart. Search me for signs of discontent. Am I living a life of contentment in you and all you provide? Or am I ungrateful and longing after the stuff of this world that I don't have? Help me, Lord, to meet my ego needs for comfort and prestige in the price your son, Jesus, paid for my redemption. God, help me to understand how debt works, both for me and against me, and help me keep a clear mind in this area. Create in me a sense of "enough," and nurture contentment in my life.

Amen.

End questions

1. *Do you agree with the statement Lynn makes that "debt is a tool, in itself neither good nor evil?" Explain your answer.*

2. *What did you learn about shopping from your family? From our culture? Are you a shopaholic – or do you know someone who is?*

3. *What does Lynn's idea of "living with enough" mean to you? How much is "enough" for you – and how do you know when you've reached it?*

4. *Read Philippians 3:7-11. What does Paul say is true gain? What is real loss? How can this guide our decisions about what is enough?*

9

An Alternative Retirement

by Lynn Miller, Stewardship Theologian, MMA

If you are like me, every once in a while you read something that makes you say, "Uh-oh!" You know, one of those things you already know but is so surprising when you see it that it almost gives you a headache from the whiplash. Recently, while reading the editorial page of a denominational magazine, I had an "uh-oh!" moment. It was an editorial about retirement, specifically about retirement communities. And the statement that jolted me was at the end of the editorial. After all the nice words about the benefits of living in a retirement center, the last words were " . . . there is no verse in the Bible describing retirement for a disciple!"

"Uh-oh!"

Not only do I live in a society fixated on being able to afford a comfortable retirement, I work for a church institution that helps people financially prepare for retirement. And frankly, now that I'm 62, I have been thinking a lot about retirement lately.

However, given the images our society presents us of retirement, I want a different word for what I am planning on doing for the rest of my life. You know the ads, the ones in *Forbes* or *Money* or *Fortune*. The ones with the silver-haired couple playing golf with palm trees in the background, or standing at the helm of a huge sailboat, or lounging on the deck of their beachfront second home. People gazing off into the distance with a look of alleged contentment on their faces.

The reality, as it nearly always is, is very different. If this couple owns a beach home on the East Coast of the United States, maybe what they are *really* gazing at in the distance is the hurricane about to sweep away their idyllic second home and sink their sailboat. Maybe that strange look on their faces is their wondering if they paid the last installment on the insurance policy for their duplicate stuff that is about to be blown away.

Okay, maybe not, but let's face it – the stereotypically "comfortable" Florida retirement might be the last act of the American Dream, but it doesn't have much to do with the life of a follower of Jesus Christ. Nothing against moving to Florida. Plenty of Christians do so. But what do you do *after* you've moved there – or wherever you retire, whether at home or some new locale?

The editor of the denominational magazine was mostly correct. Although the Levites were instructed to retire from the service in the temple and the synagogue at age 50 (Numbers 8:25), neither Jesus nor any New Testament writer said anything about retirement. Maybe that is because no one following Jesus expected to live that long! In fact, in the first century people did *not* live long enough to retire. Today as well, in most of the rest of the world, retirement is a foreign concept. Retirement comes with the wealth and leisure much of the world doesn't enjoy.

> *Retirement comes with the wealth and leisure much of the world doesn't enjoy.*

Still, we are here and this is now. Most of us will live well into our 70s, some of us into our 90s, and a few past 100. If for no other reason than the need for employment opportunities for those who follow us, retirement is a reality. But does it have to be what the American "retirement industry" wants to sell us? And is what they want to sell us what we really want? More importantly, is it what we should be seeking as Christians?

That depends on your definition of "Christian." For example, if by "Christian" you mean simply saying "yes" to Jesus and what he did for you on the cross and then just waiting around for a heavenly reward – then how you spend the rest of your life probably doesn't matter.

But, if Jesus meant what he said about who he would recognize as his followers, then we have a pretty good idea what a follower does (see Matthew 7:21). If Jesus' challenge to his disciples has anything to do with us, then taking up our crosses and denying ourselves in order to follow him is what Christians do. And if all this is true, then it makes a big difference how those of us who call ourselves Christians spend the resources – time, money, health – God has given us.

A good definition of how Christians are to spend their lives is found in Luke 4:18. Jesus enters his hometown synagogue and is given the scroll of the prophet Isaiah to read. He unrolls the scroll and finds the place where it was written: "The Spirit of the Lord is upon me, because he has anointed me to bring good news to the poor. He has sent me to proclaim release to the captive, recovery of sight to the blind, to let the oppressed go free, and to proclaim the year of the Lord's favor."

This Scripture was Jesus' job description. He brought this good news to the poor: Captives can be released, the blind can recover their sight, the oppressed are to be freed, and now is the time, the year of the Lord's favor, for release and recovery and freedom.

And this is exactly what he did immediately after leaving Nazareth. He released a man in Capernaum from an unclean demon. He freed Simon's mother-in-law from a high fever. He laid his hands on those who had various kinds of sicknesses and healed them. He began to preach, inviting repentance because God was looking to forgive. The preaching and healing was real, and all described by the Isaiah passage Jesus identified as being fulfilled in him!

Could it be that the job description of Jesus is the job description of the Christian as well? I think so — and here's why. On the front wall of the West Zion Mennonite Church in Carstairs, Alberta, Canada, in big bold letters is the best definition of the "church" I have ever seen. The inscription reads, "The Church Is the People of God Doing the Work of Jesus." The people of God doing the work of Jesus! Releasing people from captivity of all sorts, giving sight to those who are blind to what is around them, and freeing those oppressed by habits or systems or even other people. Such is the work of Jesus. It is our work, too — retired or not.

Retired Christians have a special calling in the work of Jesus because they do not need an income while they do their work. That is one of the great benefits of being retired. If you have done financial work to prepare for your retirement, you can afford to spend your time doing the work of Jesus without worrying about financial support. Consequently, retirees can afford to give away their lives doing things that pay nothing — on Earth. But, that will take a major shift in our thinking about what retirement is and what it's for.

Maybe the best way to start making that shift is to change what we call it. Instead of "retirement," which sounds like becoming "tired all over again," we could call it something more like what Jesus wants it to be.

I propose something like, *second service*. Now, second service is something I could look forward to. Something other than finding a comfortable rocking chair to sit in until I become sick enough to use the nursing home bed I now qualify for. A *second* period in life where I once again give my life away in service. A second service I pay for myself out of the abundance God has given. What more could I want? Another chance to do the work of Jesus! Let me at it!

Group questions

1. *Think about all the things you are good at. What would you enjoy doing for others if you didn't have to be paid for your time?*

2. *What would you do if you were independently wealthy?*

3. *When is it you think you will be able to begin your "second service?" At the typical retirement age of 65? A little earlier?*

Give your life away now!

You need not wait for some "magic" age to begin giving your life away. You can afford to give away the rest of your life whenever you have created an income stream that supports your needs while you are being useful in God's world.

Plus, you can give your life away a little at a time. When I was 54, I had reached the point where I didn't need to save any more money for retirement. How? I calculated that if what I had saved kept growing at a modest rate until I was 65, I would have enough to support myself and my wife without adding more to the pile. So I stopped working full-time for a full salary – and started working three-quarters time for a volunteer stipend. Nine years later, when my wife began drawing Social Security benefits, I calculated we were making about 33 percent more money than we needed, so I went from three-quarters time to half time. That means that now I have six months a year I can give away my time – without having to be paid for it!

What a blessing this is to me! I can say "yes" to all kinds of ideas and projects that come my way without regard for financial support. So far, that list includes leading learning tours to Honduras, drilling water wells in refugee villages in Central America, and building a replica of a 2,000-year-old boat in Nazareth. Some of these have already happened, some will happen in the years to come, and some may never happen. But if they don't happen, it won't be because I'm not available. I *am* available, and as long as I have the energy to take on these kinds of projects, I will. You can do this, too.

> *Say "yes" to all kinds of ideas and projects . . . without regard for financial support.*

I know a man who is using his second service years to help build a theological seminary in Guatemala City. I know others involved in the construction and maintenance of Christian camps throughout the United States. Many others regularly volunteer at nearby Habitat for Humanity projects. The funny thing is – none of those people live in a retirement community.

Now there is a truly American oddity – the "retirement community." Nowhere else in the world will you find enclaves of otherwise healthy people who willingly give up their life savings to be able to live on the outskirts of town next door to people just like them. No children, no pets, no noise – but lots of rules about where you can park and what you can plant and who can stay with you and for how long. And boy, retirement community living is expensive!

In the typical retirement community, you pay an entrance fee usually equal to the assessed value of the house or apartment you have chosen. Each year you live there, instead of seeing your equity grow as the property appreciates, you give back a portion of the equity to the retirement center. In some cases it is as much as 5 percent for 20 years; in others, it's a higher percent for a shorter time period. Either way, if you've barely managed to afford the entrance fee and then need to go into the nursing facility next door five years later, you will only have 40 percent of your initial investment. You may not have enough assets to qualify for admission.

On top of the entrance fee and the equity payments, you will pay a maintenance fee of several hundred dollars each month. You also pay your own utilities. About the only thing you don't pay is property taxes. But retirement communities exist and can charge these exorbitant fees because those who move there are desperate for community that they don't have to build or create. Instant community is expensive!

Instead, why not use retirement living as a *benefit* to an existing community – especially a dying small town? For example, I currently live four miles from a town with a one-block downtown, just off the highway. In this small town, a 6,000-square-foot, two-story building recently sold for $6,000. That's only $1 a square foot! The building sits across the street from a restaurant, the post office, a pharmacy, and a bank. Just around the corner are a dentist and a doctor's office.

Put $100,000 or so into improvements (elevator, new roof, energy efficient windows, lobby, automatic doors, etc.), and you have five or six nice apartments for $20,000-$25,000 a piece. An awning and some steel tables and chairs turns the wide sidewalk into a café. The restaurant across the street will be glad to deliver the lunches you buy from them. A video club membership and a digital projector make the lobby a movie theater for once-a-week foreign films. A small fleet of golf carts makes getting around easy. Oh, and the old basement? A great storage area.

This is not a fantasy. Right now, in this same town, a retired teacher and his wife live upstairs in a downtown commercial building they bought for $5,000!

Here is one way to become a value-added asset to an existing community. Find a small town with a small downtown, just off the main highway in a location that has a natural attraction (near one of the Great Lakes for me since I like boats). Make the town council an offer to bring a community of seniors into downtown in exchange for a zoning variation. This brings consumers into an area that has been losing them to the shopping center down the freeway – and it brings the upgrading and continued maintenance of an older building with it! Of course, there's the side benefit (for the town) of putting an abandoned building back on the tax rolls.

Here is some more good news: You may not have to pay for all of this yourself! In Sandusky, Ohio, a large town with a previously deteriorating downtown, a local developer got a grant from the Ohio Historical Society to restore and convert an old waterfront commercial building into senior housing. Now, because there are people living downtown who will use them, there are bookstores and cafés in downtown Sandusky again.

Yes, these ideas include work – but what if doing the work of Jesus includes putting together an alternative retirement setting? Dedicating yourself to a "second service?" I think it can. People are captive to their need for security and community. Offering them an alternative of living in a safe place with convenient services and retail establishments releases them from that captivity. People are often blind to their own ability to be an asset to an existing community. This idea just might give them sight to see beyond their own needs. People are often oppressed, if not depressed, by the high economic costs of retirement living facilities. This idea might be just the thing to set them free from that oppression to become an asset to a town or village slowly dying.

> *What if doing the work of Jesus includes putting together an alternative retirement setting?*

Of course, not every Christian will be able to do this exact thing. Maybe you don't have either the interest, ability, or desire to renovate and run a downtown senior living center. Or, you may be limited physically. But does the idea give you any thoughts about how your interests, abilities, and desires could be used to free captives? Bring sight to blind people? End oppression?

Are you a teacher? Free the captives of ignorance. You could tutor disadvantaged children in your subject or, thinking a little grander, you could organize a group of retired teachers to work with the local school board to provide – for free – instructional assistance to struggling students.

A lawyer? Encourage people to see the needs before them by helping those who otherwise couldn't afford it develop a will. A doctor? End the oppression that comes from chronic, yet routine, health problems faced by the indigent or homeless.

Think about what you've spent the last several years doing – or about what you'd like to do if you didn't have to worry about being paid. How could you adapt that to fit into this model? How can *your second service* be a benefit to your existing community? Let your imagination – one of your gifts from God – run wild at the thought. Brainstorm with friends who know you well. Pray about the possibilities. You'll find a niche where you can find the fulfillment that only comes with giving your life away to God.

Think about . . . what you'd like to do if you didn't have to worry about being paid.

Christians should not live according to the model of the cultural norm of society. Christians have another norm – the call to follow Jesus Christ in all we do, whether in or out of retirement. Looking for retirement alternatives begins with knowing your calling. Then you can be the church at whatever stage of life you're in.

Maybe, instead of wondering how we'll spend our "retirement" years, each of us should be asking ourselves this question: "Is Jesus the Lord of *all* my life in *all* my years?"

Prayer:

Lord, help me to see my retirement as the greatest opportunity in my life to serve you and your people. I desire to be a person who engages in the work you are doing – wherever you are doing it. I want to give my life away in service to you and I ask you, God, to show me ways to do this that will honor the gifts, abilities, talents, and desires you have placed within me. I want to follow Jesus in all I do. Give me the strength to do so with joy and gladness in my heart.

Amen.

End questions

1. *Are you intrigued by Lynn Miller's idea of a "second service," a different form of retirement? What prevents you from pursuing it? What possibilities exist near you? How can you use your set of skills, abilities, and desires in this way?*

2. *Compare the future Lynn is creating with your current retirement plans. Which one sounds most like a life given back to God?*

10

Church and Money

Note: This chapter is written as a fictional narrative, a genre often used by church-related consultants to create a more experiential way of addressing issues. It would be helpful for you to think about your own congregation as you read this. How does your congregation approach finances? The budgeting process? Does your finance board "shrink" from asking members of the congregation for money? Is your congregation "joyful" in giving?

Late afternoon sunshine poured through James Greiser's windshield as he turned into the church parking lot. James, 61, and the owner of a local restaurant, would chair the business committee meeting going on at the church.

As he entered the boardroom, James saw he was last to arrive. Already seated were Pastor Rick Coblenz, 49; Penny Moore, 45, a buyer for an apparel company; Dan Prescott, 29, newly married and serious about everything; and Susan Gorman, 37, a small business accountant.

"Since we're all here now, let's take a few moments to sit silently, gather our thoughts, and become mindful that we're about to engage in God's work," James said.

After a few moments, he prayed, asking God to guide their discussion.

"We have just one item to discuss at this meeting: our economic development proposal," James said. "As we talked last time, it is good to define our terms, and Pastor Rick has agreed to help us with this."

Pastor Rick distributed a half sheet of paper with the title, "Economic Development Proposal."

"I think we should start by defining our terms," he said. "Here are some definitions."

Economic: From the Greek "oikonomia," to be an administrator of the house. That is, the word "economic" in the title of this proposal refers to not just monetary, but to a concern for *all* assets, *all* capacities, and the care of them.

Development: To advance, further, enhance, increase, grow, broaden, mature.

Proposal: A set of organized ideas upon which we prefer to act, and about which we would like congregational permission and blessing.

"I thought we might make these definitions an introductory paragraph to the proposal," Pastor Rick continued. "I believe, from previous discussions, that these are the definitions we want to convey. We want it known that we believe God calls us to increase his kingdom – and that God chooses us as partners. The population around us is not shrinking. So, either we make room for new Christians in our facilities, or we plant another congregation, or we help other congregations grow. Either way, it requires ongoing and increased resources."

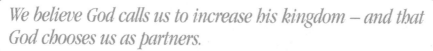

We believe God calls us to increase his kingdom – and that God chooses us as partners.

Changing definitions

As they reflected on those definitions, Susan said, "Something has your mind wandering, James. You look like you're back at the restaurant deciding what to put on the dinner menu."

James sighed, uncomfortable. "It's funny, but I have the same reaction every time we talk about this proposal. Not to assume that I'm wiser because I'm older, but I can think back over more than 40 years of church life," he said. "When I was younger, we would have been called a finance committee. Our job would have been complete if the checkbook had money in it and all church expenses were covered. No one talked about 'increasing congregational economic capacity.' We didn't even know what that meant. If someone wanted to discuss inviting more people to follow Jesus, it would be referred to a missions committee, an evangelism committee, or to people who felt evangelism was their spiritual gift."

Penny leaned forward to jump in.

"You discussed this with me earlier, James," she said, choosing her words carefully. "When I was a younger adult and first got involved in church leadership, this committee was called the stewardship and finance committee. By then, there was some understanding that watching over and generating income was as important to a congregation's fiscal health as monitoring its expenses."

Dan looked at James, then back to Penny. "I'd like to ask a question," he said. "If I understand correctly, you're saying the work of this committee has evolved. At one time it functioned like a bookkeeper. More recently like a business owner. If we are on the verge of evolving once more, what is our function now?"

Pastor Rick stepped in to answer.

"I think James was referring to a time when many congregations organized around standing committees and parliamentary procedure," he said. "Their decision-making methods were the same as those of the Rotary Club or the women's garden society.

"It wasn't until later that many congregations, including ours, adopted an enterprising model. We began to function like a nonprofit. Committees took on more active roles. Measurable outcomes began to be important. And now, for lack of a better term, we are moving to a sort of networking model."

"I understand networking conceptually when I hear it," Susan said. "But describing it to someone else is still difficult."

"I agree," Pastor Rick said. "But I think it mostly requires practice. A conversation I had recently with some other pastors may help."

Pastor Rick stood and moved to the whiteboard in the room. "Well, this group is a regular gathering of four pastors," he said. "There are other groups like it throughout the city. They are mostly pastors gathering around their common work, just like some of you do at business networking lunches."

Dan, who had lost two jobs in the last four years due to outsourcing, nodded. "Oh, yeah," he said. "Those gatherings are about the only way to make sure there is work after the next downsizing. My newest job came from networking."

Pastor Rick nodded and drew four circles on the whiteboard, each containing a number of smaller circles. "Earlier in my career, pastors rarely met across denominational lines. We met in our little circles exclusively, and were encouraged to remain at arms-length from other denominations. Anyone who got too friendly with other denominations was viewed as disloyal.

"Times have changed. The culture has shifted, but many denominations have been reluctant to follow. The result was denominations continued to offer resources that no longer met congregational needs."

"Basically," Pastor Rick said, looking at James, "the denominations were serving liver and onions to congregations hungry for pizza. And many congregations kept shoveling the liver even though they knew the people no longer wanted it and weren't eating it.

"Anyway, one of the pastors in my little group has both an MBA and his theology degree. It's an interesting mix of study, and he is one of a growing number of people seeking to combine the two disciplines."

In place of the circles, Pastor Rick wrote the words "government nonprofits" on the board.

"Government organizations get their money in annual allotments, and agencies work to spend all of their money. If they don't, they are penalized in the next budget year because of the belief that if they didn't spend it, they don't need it."

"My wife Marybelle worked for the mayor's office quite a few years," James said. "She complained about this problem every year at budget time."

Pastor Rick wrote the words "traditional nonprofits" next to his first diagram.

"Historically, nonprofits determined their expenses, then tried to raise money to meet those expenses. Our congregation did it this way for years. The problem," Pastor Rick said, "well, actually this raises at least *three* problems. The first problem is, if you don't get back to zero, you make the budget come into balance by not following through with your goals. You trim from existing programs and hope people will give more money next year.

"A second problem is that there is no forward planning and no built-in way to prioritize spending," he said. "To put it simply, you don't spend what remains unspent. Does that make sense? You end up expressing thanks to committees that didn't do their job properly and therefore didn't spend any money. How crazy is that?"

Pastor Rick was cooking now, almost like a good Sunday morning service.

"A third problem is that many congregations do a lot of asking for money without actually asking for money. They repeatedly make large group appeals but they avoid, at all costs, direct giving conversations with members. We used to do that very well, believe me."

"But we made it work," James said.

"Yes and no," Pastor Rick said. "In the past, we didn't ask people to indicate how much money they would give. Neither did we build our budget based on an income estimate. Instead, we *guessed* at the amount of money we *might* spend and hoped our general appeals would raise enough money."

He looked at James. "And what happened, James, if we were off or didn't raise enough money?"

"Well," James replied, "ultimately we trimmed something, most usually the missions budget, or we'd let the custodial contract lapse and try to keep the church clean ourselves. Things like that."

"Exactly! We changed our programming to make it meet the amount of money we had," Pastor Rick said. "We avoided, at all costs, asking people for money in any direct way, not just because we were afraid they might be offended. But also because we preferred to cut expenses when we didn't raise enough money, rather than trim expenses ahead of time to fit with an informed income projection."

Penny raised her hand. "Devil's advocate, Pastor Rick," she said. "Let's pretend I'm advocating a different point of view. I hear what you've just said, and I conclude that you don't have enough faith. You only trust in money you can see."

Pastor Rick smiled and began drawing a third diagram.

"My friend talked about that, too," he said.

"He suggested congregations move to an enterprise model and purposely keep their expenses less than their income. This way the congregation uses the remainder to cover costs when income is lower than expenses.

"But, in years where income exceeds expenses, the congregation can also carry any surplus forward into the next year. If that surplus becomes more than what a congregation needs for a cash reserve, it could be used for one-time capital, program, or mission expenses."

Pastor Rick cleared his throat a bit and looked in Penny's direction. "Now before I return to Penny's observation that this method is lacking faith, is there anything else you think a critic might say?"

"That's an easy one!" Penny laughed. "You're forgetting that the church isn't a business and you are making it one. No one should profit from the kingdom of God — but that's what your model seems to do."

"Bingo! People, we are lucky to have Penny on our board," Pastor Rick said, smiling broadly. "You are absolutely right! Those are the main objections raised to functioning in this way. We don't have to get into a battle, though," he said, holding up his hands in surrender.

Laughter rippled around the table as Penny raised her fists in a mock challenge, before shaking her head and waving at Pastor Rick to go on.

"A capacity-building enterprise model helps the congregation follow through on its goals – to actually do what the people say they want to do. An organization that lives within its means is one that disciplines itself on both the income and the outgo. When there is a funding shortfall, it spends its reserves to complete the plans it committed to God. And when income increases, it replaces its reserves for the next time a shortage occurs."

As chairman, James knew he needed to move the committee along.

"Thanks, Pastor Rick, for that, uh, vivid explanation," he said. "Essentially, you're reminding us that as we implement this proposal, we need to choose a money management system that helps us live within our means. Right?"

"Right," Pastor Rick said. "And I'm saying that we learn to be more effective as a congregation by drawing on what we learn from networking. This way of managing money is responsive. It flows and contracts as income flows and contracts."

The room was quiet for a moment – until Penny again broke the silence.

"This mixing business theory with theology like you talked about Pastor Rick, is certainly one noticeable way we are doing things differently," she said. "It wasn't that long ago we were suspicious of people who engaged in business, but also claimed to be Christian. We were happy for their donations, but we didn't want them leading the congregation's affairs."

"I don't disagree with you, Penny," James said. "But I do wonder if that isn't a little strong? Business people were asked to help with those finance committees of old, so they were in some leadership positions. It's just that we disconnected finances from the congregation's mission. We didn't understand that a congregation's economic capacity had any bearing on its calling."

"That's fine," Penny observed. "But I'm making the point that our congregation is going to require some education with this. We have people who feel like we're too progressive because we are starting to operate the way a nonprofit works. What we are discussing now shifts the ground again."

James felt everyone needed a stretch break, and he invited the group to do so. Ten minutes later, they worked out the final edits to their proposal.

Group questions

1. *Do you recognize your congregation in anything Pastor Rick was saying? If so, what?*

2. *In the content of this chapter so far, to what do you say "amen," and to what do you say "oh my?"*

An economic development proposal

Proposed by the Business Committee

Introduction: Title definitions

Economic – from the Greek "oikonomia," to be an administrator of the house. That is, the word "economic" in the title of this proposal refers to not just monetary issues, but to a concern for *all* assets, *all* capacities, and the care of them.

Development – to advance, further, enhance, increase, grow, broaden, mature.

Proposal – a set of organized ideas upon which we prefer to act, and would like permission and blessing.

Thus, we want your blessing as we increase our congregation's capacity for ministry. In recent years we have seen our congregation do less than it wanted because:

1. We ask people to consider giving a set amount of money rather than a recommended percentage of their income.

Example 1: Giving by amount: Family A contributes $1,000 to our congregation. In the next year they earn $2,000 more in income (increasing from $38,000 to $40,000) and increase giving by $100, or five percent of the additional income. Family A's annual contribution has now increased to $1,100.

Example 2: Giving by percentage: Family B earns the same amount of money and has the same increase as Family A. They also have a habit of tithing (contributing 10 percent). Their current $38,000 income means they contribute $3,800 to our church. A $2,000 increase in income means their annual contribution grows by $200 to $4,000.

2. We turn down ministry opportunities rather than asking for the money to fund them.

3. We emphasize monetary contributions more than gifts of time, possessions, and talent – which can also be used to further kingdom work. Most especially, we overlook entrepreneurial gifts that could increase our capacity.

We propose that:

1. We begin managing money based on income received rather than on anticipated expense. Our budgetary emphasis shifts to living within our means rather than trying to raise money to cover what we've already committed to spend.

2. We encourage entrepreneurial activity as a means of generating income and expanding our ministry.

3. We do not shrink from asking those who love this congregation to support it in specific ways. In the past, because we were not specific in our requests, the following occurred:

   A. Everyone felt some obligation to do everything. As a result many did nothing, and;

   B. Givers did not know where to start or stop. No volunteer fully understood his or her task or when that task was finished. Again, many did nothing as a result.

By becoming specific in our requests, we intend to create more opportunity to give and serve, especially in ways that contribute to the health and joy of this congregation.

We seek your blessing as we take these steps. We want them to be guiding principles as we begin to plan for our future. We look forward to a report next year that shows we have increased our capacity in service to God.

Prayer:

Lord, as we think about our life together as a body of believers and about the ways we want to accomplish the mission you've given us, help us to embrace change – using it to move our congregations forward in service. As members of your congregation, help us to become comfortable with discussions about money and how it can best be gathered – and distributed – in your honor.

Amen.

End questions

1. *If your congregation began to do the three things detailed in the proposal, what might become possible? Would you add to or change this list in any way?*

2. *How might these three items strengthen the invitation to more completely love and follow Christ?*

3. *What connections do you observe between faith and money in this chapter? How do you think an individual's life with both faith and money intertwines with a congregation's management of money?*

11

Faith in the Marketplace

In the previous chapter, we gained insight into how congregations are moving to link money management to ministry performance. Many are moving beyond voluntary ministry to expectations about ministry. What does this mean? It's a transformation that means congregations are moving from occasionally asking for money to meet specific needs that arise, to needing consistent giving in order to sustain the obligations of an ongoing ministry program. It also means they are often working with multiple revenue lines such as estate giving, endowments, and rental income.

There are numerous examples of congregations that link enterprise to the ministry of the church: job training programs, medical or legal clinics, schools, property management, low-income housing, even barbershops and cafés. These congregations not only have multiple lines of income, they also have multiple uses of the same dollar. A dollar spent in the café becomes a wage paid to the café worker, which in turn becomes a tithe off of their income.

> *These congregations not only have multiple lines of income, they also have multiple uses of the same dollar.*

Accounting for all this requires a greater sophistication in management than congregations needed in the past. It moves the congregation into new decision-making patterns and a need for more frequent and sophisticated patterns of communication.

Does this sound like something new and strange? It isn't.

Consider these words from Luke's account of the early church in Acts 4 "Now the full number of those who believed were of one heart and soul, and no one said that any of the things that belonged to him was his own, but they had everything in common. And with great power the apostles were giving their testimony to the resurrection of the Lord Jesus, and great grace was upon them all. There was not a needy person among them, for as many as were owners of lands or houses sold them and brought the proceeds of what was sold and laid it at the apostles' feet, and it was distributed to each as any had need" (Acts 4:32-35 ESV).

Long ago, the first congregation was pooling resources for reasons other than paying building utilities or buying Sunday school curriculum. The sources of income went beyond tithes of one's wages. Note, too, that the management of these resources rested with the apostles – the equivalent of today's multi-staffed congregations.

Congregations like these have existed for a long time and in many places. This is often how the persecuted church must function in order to survive. If mutual aid and economic inventiveness were not practiced, the persecuted church could not survive. Monasteries, communal Christian communities such as the Hutterites, and base Christian communities are also examples of congregations that pool resources, have multiple streams of income, and mingle ministry with the marketplace.

Talk to Christians with these experiences and they will share freely of Jesus as a guide for their choices. Jesus mingled in the marketplace. His stories were thoroughly seasoned with marketplace realities. Jesus invited his followers to use wealth to grow good works that introduce people to God's family (Matthew 25:14-30; Luke 16:1-13). Using wealth to grow good works doesn't always require charitable giving. Sometimes the work gets done through wise investing, ethically sound business practices, and being just toward the laborer.

Group questions

1. *The paragraph above refers to believers who feel Jesus influences them as they or their congregation engage in enterprise. Which teachings do you think they have in mind?*

2. *Are you comfortable with expressions of faith in the marketplace as advocated by congregations such as these? Why or why not?*

3. *How do you feel when a pastor is active in the marketplace or is giving counsel to people engaged in business? Do you view this mostly as a supportive act of friendship, as something pastoral, or as a means to disguise greed as something spiritual?*

The intersection between household and congregation

Congregations like these cannot place their success at the feet of fiscal savvy or creativity. Rather, their success comes from church members who organize their lives for God's use. They are creative because they keep seeking ways to do more for their Lord. Congregations such as these enjoy the benefit of people who have moved beyond tithing to a tighter integration of all their resources in service to God. They seek to use their homes, their labor, their family activities, their need to purchase goods and services, and even the distribution of their estates in ways that further the ministry of their congregation.

Here is an example: The congregation our family attends has both a café staffed by volunteers and a Saturday night service – the service we generally attend. We come early, stay late, and usually buy dinner in the café. Thus, the money we might normally spend in a restaurant remains in our congregation. Our time, our talents, and the money under our management are more tightly organized for the Lord's use.

People who organize their lives like this drive down a lifestyle stake – and stay there. They have no need for a larger home or a new car so they do not buy them. They enjoy life. They indulge their passions, but avoid conspicuous consumption. Their income goes up over the years, but they keep their expenses down. This lets them increase their savings rate (which helps them grow in cash flow and in assets) and also increase their giving. It is their delight to show gratitude to God, by giving 10 percent and beyond, but their desire to grow in giving moves beyond even this.

They sponsor orphans in other countries. They encourage their children to volunteer. They get involved in youth sports programs, or join the Chamber of Commerce, or take groceries to shut-ins. Without people like these, congregations could not continue in creative ministry. Most non-profit organizations would also collapse for lack of volunteers.

People like this are not out for praise or awards. They believe giving is its own investment – and reward. They believe what they share with their family, their community, and the world strengthens the bonds of friendship and builds goodwill so that others take up a life of generosity. The result of their investment is a wealth of family and friends.

Giving is its own investment – and reward.

People like this also have no debt as they move into the last phase of their careers and then into retirement. This allows them to increase their giving yet again.

Let's return to James Greiser from the last chapter, the nearly retired restaurant owner. Pretend that the economic proposal his congregation was considering is put into place and James is now ready to retire. He has sold his restaurant, but because of the lifestyle stake he drove years ago he doesn't need the proceeds of the sale to fund his retirement. Because he has lived a long life of growing in generosity, in cash flow, and in assets, he is eager to continue honoring God in some way. Since he doesn't need the money, he decides to do something better with it.

With the permission of his congregation, he purchases and rehabilitates an old warehouse, constructing 15 low-cost condominiums for seniors that his congregation will manage. James and his wife will live in one of the apartments. Another apartment will house an on-site nurse who will assist with home health care needs. Since the building is already paid for by James, the purchase price of each condominium is lowered and can be pooled to pay the nurse's salary and to endow maintenance expenses.

Why not take up the challenge to live your life in this way? Why not do something grand and meaningful? Why not do something, because life does not belong to you alone? Do something wonderful with what you have, because life will continue in your descendants after you leave this world. Take up this challenge to be magnanimous – and leave more behind than you were given.

> *Why not do something grand and meaningful?*

The 3 R's

Many congregations dream of engaging in ministry in this way, but cannot seem to move beyond the dream. That is because the aspirations of the people must move from the standard upwardly mobile lifestyle to a lifestyle of incarnational ministry.

Years ago, a congregation I pastored initiated one of the first ministries in our city for latchkey children. Our church building sat within walking distance of five elementary schools in an inner-city neighborhood. A number of children spent their afternoons on the streets until their parents came home from work, if their parents had jobs at all.

As we began working more intentionally with these children and their families, offering tutoring services in cooperation with the nearby schools, we discovered we needed help. The leaders of our congregation began to study a book written by John Perkins.[1] This book taught us about the three R's of community ministry.

Relocation. Perkins wrote that relocating to a community is one way we could teach about the incarnate Christ – coming and living among us. He said it is hard to be taken seriously or to be effective if you try to minister from a distance. Prior to that time, our congregation drove to the neighborhood to minister. Within a few years, more of our members had relocated to the neighborhood. We were able to continue in ministry in informal ways and with formal programs.

Reconciliation. Reconciliation, according to Perkins, means working at healing relationships – between people as well as between people and the God who created them.

Redistribution. This principle is learning to share with your neighbors. Learning to share your hearth and home, skill and substance.

Relocation – the first R – helps redistribution become something more than charitable giving. It becomes something that builds community.

Our congregation learned then, as I hope to convey now, that a congregation which intends to live within its means in order to grow in generous ministry, is built on people who also live within their means – in all aspects of life.

Prayer:

Lord, help us to continue efforts to encourage our congregations to operate as a New Testament church, in ways that will advance your kingdom. Though we know how important individual tithes are, help us, God, to supplement our giving to you with pursuing alternative sources of income. Guide us, Lord, as we set lifestyle stakes that allow us to give more and more of ourselves and our lives to you. Help us, God, to find ways to be magnanimous in our communities, sharing all aspects of the rich and bountiful lives you have provided.

Amen.

End questions

1. Read the following texts and note what these stories hold in common: Luke 19:1-9; 23:50-56; and 2 Corinthians 8:1-5. How do these texts illuminate this chapter?

2. How would the three R's (relocation, reconciliation, and redistribution) relate to the community where your congregation is located?

3. Pursuing the three R's changes the way a congregation manages money. Specifically, it is more likely to manage money as an enterprise than as a volunteer organization. What are the strengths of such an adjustment? What weaknesses would you expect? Do you think a congregation can become more enterprising without changing its style of managing money?

Sources

1   John Perkins, "With Justice for All," Zondervan, 1981.

12

Finishing Well

When my father was 55, he asked me to serve as the executor of his estate. He and my mother had just completed their wills and were putting their affairs in order. Their prior planning will make my job mostly a formality.

At age 35, my wife was diagnosed with a rare form of cancer. She and I used the occasion to update our wills, establish power of attorney for each other, initiate an estate trust, and sign our Do Not Resuscitate orders at our local hospital. We have it all orchestrated now. If we live to see our children to adulthood, all of our estate will go to charity when we die. For a time it will be put into a trust, with the interest paid to our children and/or grandchildren, but in 20 years or so, all of the principle will go to the charities we've named.

An elderly man recently spoke with me, just two weeks from an estate sale of the two farms he owns. He and his wife are moving to a church-related nursing home in another community. Once all their affairs are settled, he intends to leave a substantial gift to the congregation he contributed to all his life.

Life is so fragile and can end so suddenly. Examples like these remind us that there is only one way to fulfill our plans for the end of our lives – and that is to make plans in the first place. When no plans are made, our survivors grieve more deeply. They end up having to put our affairs in order because we never got around to it. This is difficult when a survivor is also trying to accept what it means to live without you.

> *There is only one way to fulfill our plans for the end of our lives – and that is to make plans in the first place.*

It gets even worse if your instructions – and your desires – are not known. Too often, children, spouses, and even grandchildren end up estranged from each other over differences in how they think your estate should be managed.

The size of your estate has little bearing on these conflicts, by the way. Conflicts grow over sentimental objects, over what is sold and what remains intact, and also over how possessions are divided. The intense conflict can be over a handful of diamonds – or a $5 piece of jewelry.

MMA considers having a will so important that they have a program to provide up to $50 to help Anabaptist church members create or update a will. To learn more about that, contact your local MMA counselor, the advocate at your church, or call MMA at (800) 348-7468.

But, you need to know that it is never too late to get started. Some people delay because they feel they can't afford the money it would cost them to draft a will. However, a will can be very affordable. Many denominational foundations and some Christian community foundations provide an inexpensive service to craft a basic will. Even if you discover your estate is complicated enough that a lawyer is needed, having a will saves your estate a lot of money in the long run. Lawyer costs now are much cheaper than probate costs later.

Group questions

1. Have you written your will? Is it current? Does it include a power of attorney?

2. Have you determined how you want end-of-life issues handled? Do you have this on file with your physician and/or hospital? Does your family know about your plans?

More than a will

Getting your will in place is a great start, but many people need more technical help. This is where having conversations with an MMA counselor, competent estate planner, and/or foundation officer can be most helpful. These professionals are in the best position to assist you with the goals you have for your estate.

Some Christians remain uncomfortable with the word "goals" – especially when talking about their estate. They are afraid of sounding materialistic and focused on this life instead of the life to come. But this is not about getting rich. Your goals ought to be focused on growing in cash flow, assets, and giving – just as they are now in your life. Your goals aren't "growth targets." Instead, they're a list of what you want in place as you age and eventually die.

Meeting with an experienced professional helps you determine who or what receives your assets after you die. The professional can help identify the financial instruments needed to make this possible. If you fail to plan and get these instruments in place, your state will determine the distribution of your estate for you. If this happens, they will assess your estate for the cost – and the government doesn't work cheap! Taxes and legal fees will leave far less for those you love and the charities you supported than if you completed planning yourself.

Some people avoid these decisions because they feel it is morbid – or they want to delay thinking about death. They end up putting it off until it is too late. They don't complete their estate plans because it feels like they are picking out their flowers, hymns, and burial plot.

> *They don't complete their estate plans because it feels like they are picking out their flowers, hymns, and burial plot.*

United States and Canadian tax laws actually encourage you to plan your estate and to avoid paying taxes and legal fees. By completing your plan and the related documents yourself, you dictate who or what receives how much and when. These laws even encourage you to leave money to both charity and your heirs.

This is what my wife and I plan to do. When we turn 65, we intend to donate all of our investments to a church-related foundation. The foundation will turn this donation into a trust instrument of some sort that will pay us an interest percentage on the principle. Anything earned above the agreed-upon percentage will be given to the charities we name. After our death, the percentage will go either to our children or grandchildren (depending on how long we live) for 20 years. When those years are up, the entire principle is given to the charities we name.

In this way, we will receive a fixed income, and there will be an inheritance to pass on to our descendants. Plus, charities we love will continue to receive from us throughout and beyond.

Giving beyond your will

Gift plan	How it works
Bequest	Name Mennonite Foundation as a beneficiary in your will. File a bequest plan with Mennonite Foundation recommending charities to receive your donations at death. Can change at any time without changing your will.
Charitable gift annuity	Donate cash or other assets to Mennonite Foundation, which makes guaranteed payments to you for life. At death, the balance goes to charities you recommend.
Charitable gift fund	Donate assets to Mennonite Foundation, which sells them for you. Get an immediate income tax deduction, avoid capital gains tax, and recommend the charities to receive your donations over time.
Charitable remainder unitrust	Donate assets to Mennonite Foundation, which sells them for you. Get an immediate income tax deduction, avoid capital gains tax, and receive variable payments for life. Recommend the charities that benefit from the remaining balance.
Charitable remainder annuity trust	Donate assets to Mennonite Foundation, which sells them for you. Get an immediate income tax deduction, avoid capital gains tax, and receive guaranteed payments for life. Recommend the charities that benefit from the remaining balance.
Charitable remainder lead trust	Donate assets to Mennonite Foundation. Recommend charities to receive payments for a period of time, then the asset returns to you.

Each estate is different, of course. Estate planners and church-related foundations, such as Mennonite Foundation, have a variety of tools and can draw on them to assist you with your specific goals. Foundation officers work for you, helping to carry out your wishes according to your values. In many cases, the officer will visit you at your request, working with you regardless of the size of your estate – even if the only thing you own is your home.

It can be difficult to admit your life is changing, but change happens to us all. If you embrace this natural course of events, it becomes easier to plan where your estate will ultimately be distributed. Given the alternative of grieving family members having to figure out what your estate contains, guessing what your intentions were, and then going to court to get permission to carry them out, why not embrace change and complete your plans now, while you can? That doesn't sound so bad after all.

Finish well so that your descendants can begin strong.

Prayer:

God, we acknowledge that all we have comes from you and we proclaim
our desire to "finish well" so those who follow after us can live well.
Help us, Lord, to bear in mind that life is fragile and we are not
guaranteed tomorrow. Help us to view death as a healthy part of life,
and encourage us as we prepare for both, keeping your
guidance at the front of our considerations.
Amen.

End questions

1. Do you have an estate plan? Is it current?

2. Completing an estate plan requires that you speak openly about money and how you handled it during your lifetime. With whom are you free to have such a conversation?

3. What steps have you taken to live an exemplary life and finish well? What steps do you need to take? How will you do so?

4. Looking back over this book, identify one significant insight you gained and one remaining question you would like to ask.

To ask your questions, contact:
MMA
1110 North Main St.
P.O. Box 483
Goshen, IN 46527

Toll-free: (800) 348-7468
Telephone: (574) 533-9511
www.mma-online.org

Final Word: The Other Side

The stewardship of money is a complex issue. No wonder Jesus spoke so often about money and its spiritual connections. He knew its allure would challenge the hearts of God's people. That certainly hasn't changed.

And in our culture today – the wealthiest society in the history of humankind – money's allure challenges us ever more frequently and on increasingly deeper levels than we have ever known before. We have so much. Yet, we often think we have so little. A missionary, commenting on America's unprecedented wealth, once said that "America's greatest need is she has no need."

The truth of that assertion is convicting, isn't it? Yet, it's not entirely true. Because America does have one great, overriding need – the need to be faithful to God. As Jesus warned in the Sermon on the Mount, we cannot serve both God and money (Matthew 6:24). We must choose which god will receive our allegiance and devotion. How we steward the money given us speaks more clearly than any of our words about which god we choose.

Mark Vincent, along with different MMA staff members, has provided a helpful framework for talking about money stewardship that honors God with this book. The testimony of the Macedonian church that opened this study (2 Corinthians 8:1-5) still speaks to the local church today. Are we giving first to God? Are we giving what we are able to give? Are we being as generous in sharing God's good gifts (James 1:17) as God has been in sharing the best gift of all – Jesus – with us?

Money is not a financial issue. It is a spiritual issue. Money is not about your bank account. It is about your heart for God and others. Money is not about quantity. It is about the quality of life it can bring. It is a gift from God that can be used for many greater goals. May this study start you on, or take you further down, the road of managing money for the One who owns it all anyway (Psalm 37:21).

– *Steve Ganger, MMA Director of Stewardship Education*

Bringing stewardship to life

If you enjoyed Money Mania: Mastering the Allure of Excess, you will want to consider the other books in MMA's Living Stewardship study series, including **"Time Warped: First Century Time Stewardship for 21st Century Living."**

In "Time Warped", Steve Ganger, MMA's director of stewardship education, provides:

- Twelve flexible, interactive lessons on how to "do less" yet create a more fufilling relationship with God.

- Practical Scriptural applications that ground each lesson in God's Word.

- Personal time chart and planning documents that help you take immediate action.

- Helpful group discussion questions that encourage deep, personal reflection.

- Encouragement and ideas that will motivate you to make lasting life changes now!

MMA's Living Stewardship study series examines holistic stewardship from the inside out in the areas of time, talents, money, health, and relationships. Each book deals with one area of stewardship – but in a holistic way.

You will think about stewardship in new ways as you work through these titles – and more books are in the planning stages now! Visit MMA-online (www.mma-online.org) to learn more about holistic stewardship.

Living Stewardship books and other educational resources, are available in the MMA Bookstore (www.bookstore.mma-online.org) or call (800) 348-7468, Ext. 269.

Bringing stewardship to life

If you enjoyed Money Mania: Mastering the Allure of Excess, you will want to consider the other books in MMA's Living Stewardship study series, including **"Talent Show"** *coming in the fall.*

In his book on talents, Bob Lichty, an MMA marketing manager with a heart for gifts discernment, provides:

- Twelve flexible, interactive lessons on how to use your spiritual gifts, talents, passions, style, and experience to take action for God.

- Practical Scriptural applications that ground each lesson in God's Word.

- A comprehensive spiritual gifts assessment.

- Helpful group discussion questions that encourage deep, personal reflection.

- Encouragement and ideas that will motivate you to make lasting life changes now!

MMA's Living Stewardship study series examines holistic stewardship from the inside out in the areas of time, talents, money, health, and relationships. Each book deals with one area of stewardship – but in a holistic way.

You will think about stewardship in new ways as you work through these titles – more books are in the planning stages now! Visit MMA-online (www.mma-online.org) to learn more about holistic stewardship.

Living Stewardship books and other educational resources, are available in the MMA Bookstore (www.bookstore.mma-online.org) or call (800) 348-7468, Ext. 269.

Resources from Lynn Miller

MMA's stewardship theologian, Lynn Miller, has helped countless people shape a vision for holistic stewardship that includes their time, talents, money, health, and relationships. His books and other resources will stimulate your thinking.

"Firstfruits Living": The book that started it all! "Firstfruits Living" teaches that God calls all people to make their lives an offering to God. Also available as a video series of 10 study lessons for small groups or Sunday school classes.

"Just in Time": In his second book, Lynn shows, through stories, what happens when we make ourselves an offering to God.

"The Power of Enough": Lynn challenges the assumption of materialism that happiness can be found in material possessions. Also available on CD as an audio series of 10 study lessons for small groups or Sunday school classes.

Let Lynn Miller challenge your thoughts on holistic stewardship! Visit MMA-online (www.mma-online.org) to learn more. Lynn's books and other resources are available in the MMA Bookstore (www.bookstore.mma-online.org) or call (800) 348-7468, Ext. 269.

Other resources from Mark L. Vincent

Mark L. Vincent works to strengthen generosity in congregations and families. His experiences in the pastorate, denominational leadership, and in business enhance his unique ability to help ministries face tough money issues. His books and other resources will make you think about money from a new perspective.

"Speaking About Money": Through stories, questions, and practical guidelines, Mark provides insight and tools for reducing the tension surrounding public discussions about money and faithful stewardship.

"A Christian View of Money": How you live is an accurate representation of what you believe, according to Mark. This is particularly seen in a Christian's use of money. This book provides an essential theological undergirding to discussions about money.

"Faithful and Wise": Ask most Christians what the word "stewardship" means and you will likely get answers that talk about money. But, thinking holistically, money is just one of the gifts God gives us to use for his glory. Mark narrates this video which looks at ways to expand our concept of giving.

If you enjoyed "Money Mania: Mastering the Allure of Excess", let Mark continue to challenge your thoughts on money issues! Mark's resources are available in the MMA Bookstore (www.bookstore.mma-online.org) or call (800) 348-7468, Ext. 269.

Date D